Bronze Age
America

OTHER BOOKS BY BARRY FELL

Life, Space and Time

America B.C.

Saga America

Bronze Age America

BARRY FELL

LITTLE, BROWN AND COMPANY

BOSTON   TORONTO

Library of Congress Catalog card no. 82-47515

First Edition

ISBN 0-316-27771-1

Published simultaneously in Canada
by Little, Brown & Company (Canada) Limited

Printed in the United States of America

THIS IS A RUGGLES DE LATOUR, INC., BOOK · NEW YORK

Frontispiece page 1. An unnamed goddess (probably Sulis) mounted upon a deer (*see page 231*). *Frontispiece page
3.* Norse iron battle-axe from Massachusetts coast (*see
page 180*). *Frontispiece page 4.* A Celt, executed in bedrock, discovered at Searsmont, Maine (*see page 98*).

CONTENTS

ACKNOWLEDGMENTS

This book is an expansion of materials presented originally in the University Lecture Series at the University of Miami in 1982, under the title *Bronze Age America: The Nordic Settlements.*

Dr. William P. Grigsby, aided by Edna Bishop, selected inscribed stone and bone artifacts from his collections made in Tennessee and adjacent states, and also made available skeletal materials from the same burials as those from which many of the artifacts were excavated. Ruth K. Hanner, librarian of the Epigraphic Society, located some of the relevant literature, especially on Scandinavian inscriptions. Radiocarbon dating was carried out by Geochron Laboratories, Cambridge, Massachusetts. Vernon J. Calhoun supplied valuable information on Kentucky sites, and Edward R. Moore on the ancient copper mines of Lake Superior. James P. Whittall, Malcolm Pearson and their colleagues of the Early Sites Research Society provided information and photographs of their materials, mainly from the northeastern sites. Field photography was carried out by Otto Devitt, latterly assisted by Russell Tilt, at the Peterborough site; Dr. Julian Fell in Alberta, and Wayne and Betty Struble at the Tule Lake site, contributed many photographs, as did my companions in the field John Williams, Peter Garfall and Dr. Jon Polansky. For access to his records, and for valuable discussion, I am indebted to the late Professor Robert Heizer. Gloria Farley made available latex peels from her explorations, and assisted greatly in gaining information on sites in Oklahoma and adjacent states. Numerous photographs were supplied by members of the Epigraphic Society.

For these, and other contributions individually acknowledged in the captions or the text, I am deeply grateful.

Harvard University
Cambridge
and
The Epigraphic Society,
6625 Bamburgh Drive
San Diego

INTRODUCTION

My purpose in this book is to make known a remarkable discovery that demonstrates that a Scandinavian king made a voyage to America around 1700 B.C., to barter textiles with the Algonquian Indians in return for metallic copper ingots. He left a detailed record of his visit and makes it clear that before he returned to his capital near the head of Oslo Fjord, he established a permanent trading colony. I also take the opportunity of further developing the ideas set out in my previous books: that Europeans during the Bronze Age were literate, educated people, who have left engraved rock inscriptions, recording their Teutonic and Celtic tongues, using alphabets that have survived to this very day in remote parts of the world, though these alphabets died out two thousand years ago in Europe, when the Roman script became the predominant alphabet of our ancestors.

To most archaeologists, both in Europe and in America, such notions appear preposterous. There was no writing in Scandinavia until about the time of Christ, they say, and hence it is impossible to discover what language the people of the Bronze Age spoke, and even more absurd (so many American archaeologists add) to suppose that the Bronze Age peoples of Europe could have ever visited America.

To demonstrate the error of such claims, first glance at the two alphabets set out in Figure I-1. One of these, called *ogam consaine,* is a way of writing used by the Celts and recorded and explained in detail by Irish monks during the Middle Ages. As I have already given a full account of it in *America B.C.* and *Saga America,* there is no need to discuss it further at this point, except to note that encyclopedias *usually* state that ogam was "invented in London

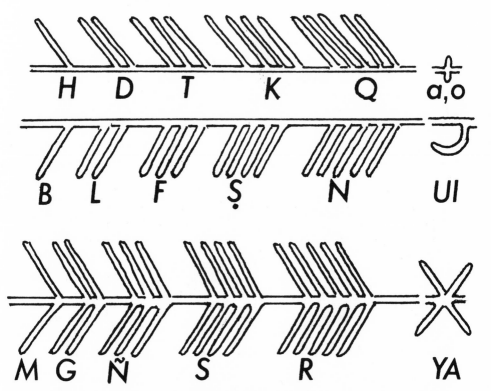

Figure I-1. Early form of the ogam consaine alphabet, in which only consonants are expressed, plus the diphthong *ui* and a semivowel, *ya*. Inscriptions in this alphabet occur in many countries and also on the pre-Roman silver coinage of the Gauls. Use of the ogam alphabet was suppressed in Roman colonies by the Lex Coloniae of the Roman code of laws, passed in 133 B.C., but a temporary revival of ogam on Iberian coins occurred in A.D. 2 under Augustus. In rare instances a sign for *a* or *o* is used in King Woden-lithi's inscriptions.

Variant forms are numerous. In *fringe ogam* the strokes all stand upon, or hang from, the same axis, but vary in length, as shown. This type of ogam is usually written on the outlines of pictographs.

around the fourth century A.D. by a person familiar with Latin." If the statement were true, it would have been impossible for anyone at all to have written ogam before Roman times. The other alphabet, called *Tifinag,* is the special way of writing of the Tuaregs, a race of Berbers living in the Atlas Mountains in North Africa. Both ogam consaine and Tifinag use only consonants in nearly all words, leaving the vowels to be inferred, as do writers of Hebrew, Arabic, and other ancient scripts. Occasionally, where doubt may exist as to the word intended, a vowel sign is added, or a pictograph, to help recognize the word.

Having these two alphabets in hand, we may now examine some of the famous Bronze Age sites where rock-cut inscriptions are preserved. One of the most convenient is at Hjulatorp, in Sweden. The name of the place means "Wheel Village," and undoubtedly Hjulatorp takes its name from the presence there of a series of rock carvings that resemble chariot wheels, and others that look like disks or globes (Figures I-3 to I-5). Archaeologists state that these are the work of either late Neolithic or early Bronze Age sculptors—and I agree with that opinion. Now examine the fernlike inscription on the lower part of the rock face, beneath some circular carvings. You will have little difficulty in recognizing this as ogam consaine, and that the letters are as shown on Figure I-3. They spell K-UI-G-L, which, as all Nordic- and German-speaking readers will immediately recognize, is just an archaic way of spelling the general Teutonic root that means a ball or globe. Glance now to the upper right, where, beside the same circular images, we now find a series of engraved dots that match letters in the Tifinag alphabet. The letters are, as shown in Figure I-4, K-G-L—again, just an archaic rendering of the same word, this time in a different alphabet. There are more of the Tifinag letters. Look at the chariot wheels to the right of the globes (Figure I-5). Beneath them are letters that spell W-H-L-A, obviously an archaic spelling of the old Norse word for wheel. Farther to the right we find a Tifinag word spelling K-L. Now the writer of that last word may have been an ancient Swede, already casting out from his pronunciation of *kugl* that internal *g,* for whereas Danes and Germans retain the internal consonant, the Swedes now spell and pronounce *kugl* as *kula.*

But, you say, there is not supposed to be any writing at all

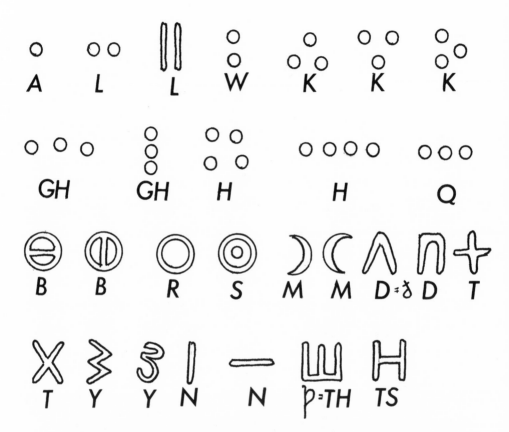

Figure I-2. Forms of letters used in the Tifinag alphabet, originally used by the white Berbers (Tuaregs) of North Africa, but now adopted by a number of non-Berber tongues in Northwest Africa. Among books printed in this Braille-like script may be mentioned parts of the four Gospels. Rock-cut inscriptions range back to pre-Roman times in Africa.

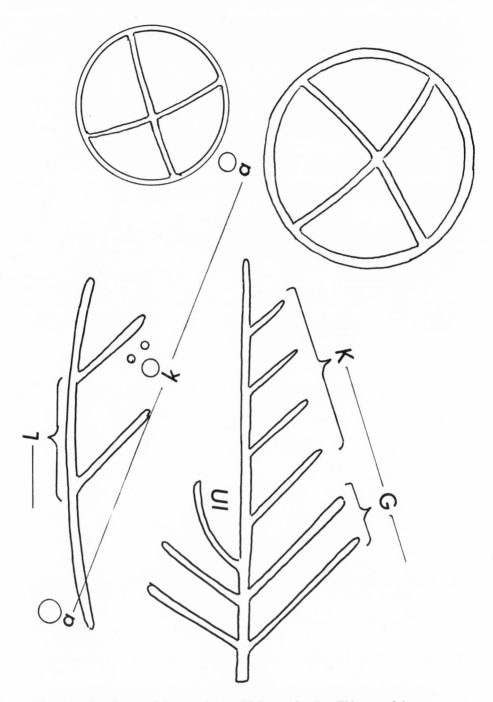

Figure I-3. The figures of the sun globe at Hjulatorp, Sweden. This part of the ancient inscription is written in ogam consaine (K-UI-G-L, globe) and Tifinag (A-K-A, drives), and states evidently that the globe of the sun god drives across the sky in a chariot. Other similar texts refer to the sun and the moon as sailing sky ships. The language is recognizable as an archaic form of Old Norse.

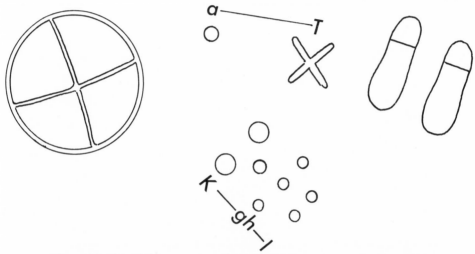

Figure I-4. The Old Norse text continues on the Hjulatorp inscription, to the right of the part shown in Figure I-3, by designating on the stone in Tifinag letters T-A K-GH-L, *Tá kughla*, "the path of the [sun's] globe." A relic of the still older Neolithic hieroglyphic script persists in the ideogram of a pair of shoe-prints, representing the word *tá*, "path." Thus the Hjulatorp inscription as a whole has reference to the path of the sun across the sky, and was probably the site of a calendar-regulation observatory. See Chapter 5 for an account of the Bronze Age calendar-regulation observatory set up by King Woden-lithi in Ontario, before he returned to Ringerike in Norway.

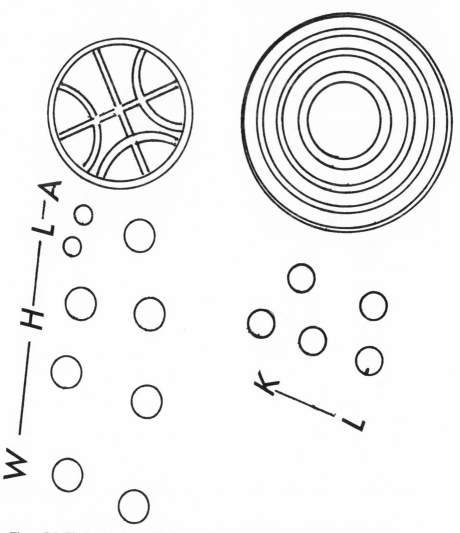

Figure I-5. The inscription at Hjulatorp, Sweden, continues, with these elements to the right of those shown in Figure 4. The archaic Norse word for wheel appears beside what is evidently a chariot wheel, and below another disk K-L, presumably the dialectal shortening of *kugl*, a globe.

on these Bronze Age monuments! Well, that is not now my opinion, and I suspect it is beginning to occur to you that perhaps our earlier ideas may have erred on these matters. Now let us take a look at another Bronze Age carving, first recorded by Dr. G. Halldin in the 1949 volume of the yearbook published by the Swedish Sjöfartsmuseum. It shows a ship of the characteristic Bronze Age form, with the keel projecting fore and aft below the upward-turned bow and stern pieces. Along the upper and lower borders of the uppermost ship (Figure I-6) we see two lines of Tifinag letters, and a third line curves around the lower edge of the rock slab. In the Bronze Age (and also among the Berbers in modern times), when two or more lines of text occur, they are read as if they were a continuous "tape": that is, with each line alternating in direction, so that no break occurs in the line of symbols. Here we read the top line from left to right, the next line from right to left. The letters prove to be K-GH H-W-L. Now take a glance at an American rock inscription, also depicting ships of the Bronze Age type (Figure I-7). This particular carving, at Peterborough, Ontario, can be visited easily by Canadians living in that area, whom I now invite to join us. As can be seen, the letters K-GH occur at the beginning of the first line, too, which also is to be read from left to right, just as in the Swedish example. Reference to any Old Norse or Old Icelandic dictionary will disclose that *kuggr,* often anglicized in Viking times as *cog,* is an Old Norse word meaning a seagoing trading ship. On the Swedish example the next word, H-W-L, can readily be recognized, since it still occurs in all Nordic tongues, as meaning whale, or, in the older sense, any sea monster or leviathan. Thus the Swedish example is telling us that the monument is dedicated to "the seagoing ship *Leviathan.*" As for the Canadian examples, merely note that *kuggr* is only one of several Old Norse words for ships that we find represented by Tifinag letters beside carvings of Bronze Age ships.

Returning to Sweden, we now visit at Backa, Brastad, another site, considered by Swedish archaeologists, to be Neolithic (around 2000 B.C.). The word *backa* does not occur in modern speech, but in Old Norse it meant, according to my *Oxford Dictionary of Old Icelandic,* "a kind of blunt-headed arrow." The rock inscription that occurs at Backa depicts just such a blunt-headed arrow, together with an image of the sun god and a human figure,

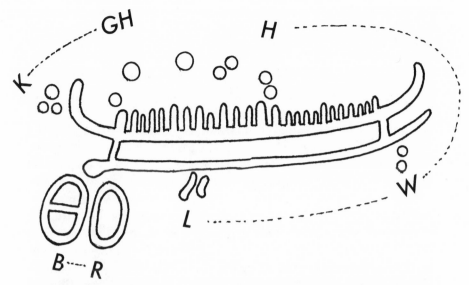

Figure I-6. Detail from a Bronze Age ship petrogylph originally published by the Sjöfartsmuseum (Halldin, 1941). The Tifinag inscription reads clockwise to yield an archaic Nordic text matching Old Norse *kogge hval*, while the large letters BR are a relic of late Neolithic hieroglyphs depicting a buckler, *bukla*, and a ring, *hringr*; these, the first of what became the Tifinag letters, were originally to be read as a punning simulation of words meaning "thrust out [to sea] at launching." (See Chapter 16.) Thus, the whole inscription is probably a memorial to the launching of the seagoing ship *Leviathan*.

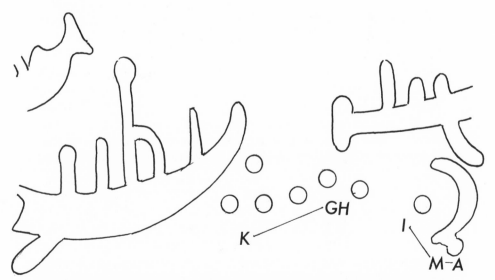

Figure I-7. America's first recorded sea battle, fought between rival flotillas of Norse cogs, is depicted in petroglyphs carved some 18 feet to the southwest of the central sun-god figure on King Woden-lithi's monument at Peterborough, Ontario. In this detail two cogs are about to clash head-on, the ship on the right apparently fitted with a battering ram, as also is the bow of the uppermost vessel to the left. The inscription reads K-GH I-M, *kogga ima*, "battle of the seagoing ships."

apparently dead, plus some letters of the Tifinag alphabet (Figure I-8). These, if read from right to left, yield the words S-L B-K-S, *solbakkas,* translating as "of the sun's blunt arrow." The precise reference may be obscure, but it seems clear enough that the letters are indeed Tifinag, and that the subject under discussion is indeed the blunt arrow that is depicted below the letters and that gave its name to the place where the inscription occurs.

The examples cited so far come from the eastern parts of Sweden and comprise very simple texts, using only a few letters of the Tifinag alphabet. If we transfer our attention to the rock inscriptions found on the southwest coast of Sweden, immediately adjacent to Oslo Fjord and along the strip of coast to the north of Göteborg, we find much more extensive and varied inscriptions at localities in the Bohuslän region. Here the texts are longer and more interesting and, in many cases, they show the same obvious relationship to the accompanying carvings of men, animals, and ships. What have hitherto been incomprehensible "lines of dots" now assume quite clearly and unmistakably the character of commentaries in a very ancient kind of Norse language that was evidently spoken during the Bronze Age. Since there was at that time no differentiation of the ancestors of the future Angles and Saxons from the general stock of Teutonic speakers that later gave rise to the tribes that spread from Denmark to England, I shall use here the terms *Nordic* and *Ancient Nordic* for the language that is represented in these Bronze Age inscriptions. It is my impression that English, German, and other Teutonic languages, including the Norse or Scandinavian tongues, may all be traced back to the Bronze Age dialect that is the subject of this chapter.

The inscriptions in western Sweden seem to fall broadly into three main categories. These are (1) short didactic statements that appear to be school lessons for young scribes, very much resembling the Celtic school inscriptions reported from British Columbia in my book *Saga America,* (2) prayers for the safety of ships at sea and for victory in impending attacks upon foes, and (3) narrative material depicting and identifying important events, such as the pagan festivals with their associated rituals and entertainments. In deciphering these Tifinag texts, from which the vowels, of course, are usually

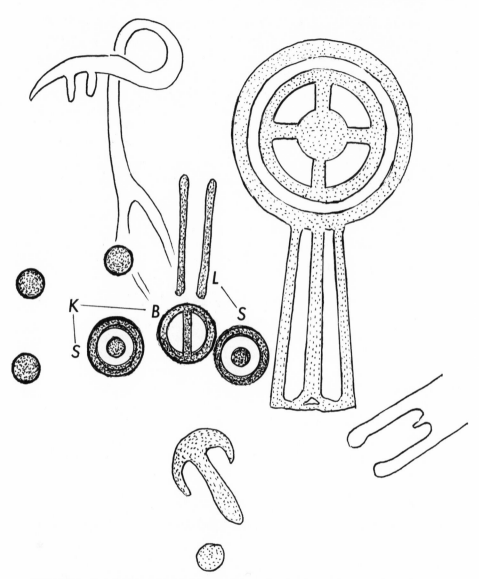

Figure I-8. Inscription at Backa, Brasted, Sweden. Tifinag letters spell out the name of the depicted "blunt arrow," apparently a religious solar concept.

lacking, I have used as my reference the known vocabulary of Old Norse and Old Icelandic. However, in many cases dialects such as Old English or Old High German could equally well be used as the reference guide, with the same translation resulting, and with little more than the substituted vowels to distinguish the various dialects. Since the vowels are lacking we are left without any certain indication as to which of the Old Teutonic tongues is the closest to the speech of these ancient Nordic people, and it is possible that all are equally related, as I suggest above. But to provide a uniform nominal vocabulary I select Old Norse or Old Icelandic as the base.

School Lessons

Any literate community has to provide a means of instructing the young in the arts of reading and writing; otherwise the skills would die out. It appears that in Bronze Age times the schoolmasters used much the same kind of didactic material for their lessons as did teachers in later ages. The subject matter ranges from simple identifications of depictions of objects of daily life to more sophisticated proverbs and adages, each illustrated by appropriate pictorial carvings.

Figure I-9 illustrates two inscribed petroglyphs from the Bohuslän district that suggest that they were intended for younger readers. The first imparts a moral lesson on cooperation; the second is of the familiar grade-school type, in which people are related to their daily environment, in this case two fishermen who are "on the water." Figure I-10 shows more of the same type of illustrated statement, in which a warrior holds his buckler in such a manner as to show how the word is spelled; a bull and a cow are introduced, each illustrating how its name is spelled; and the sun god carries the image of the sun, thus showing how the letter *s* (for *sol,* sun) originated.

Figure I-11 could also be used in teaching youngsters, though the context from which these ship details are taken suggests that it is a record of a naval episode. The ships' names are given, sometimes (as in the upper example) with a helpful hieroglyph add-

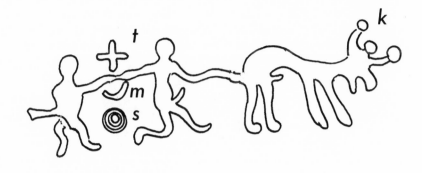

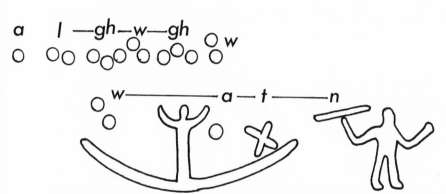

Figure I-9. School lessons from ancient Scandinavia. Above, Bronze Age of Bohus-län. A bull and two men form a team to drag some heavy object. The Tifinag letters S-M-T-K are the consonants of the Old Norse word *samtak*, meaning "united effort." Below, a detail of a Bronze Age composition at Finntorp, Bohuslän, depicting two fishermen and their boat. The Tifinag letters are probably to be read as matching the Old Norse *I loegfaki vid vatn*, "fishermen on the water." Evidently the Tifinag letter *w* sometimes represents Old Norse *v*, and sometimes Old Norse *f*. The phonetic rendering yielded by reading the Tifinag letters often seems closer to Anglo-Saxon, where the sound *w* replaced the *v* of Norse, and modern dialects of Jutland in west Denmark also retain the *w* sound.

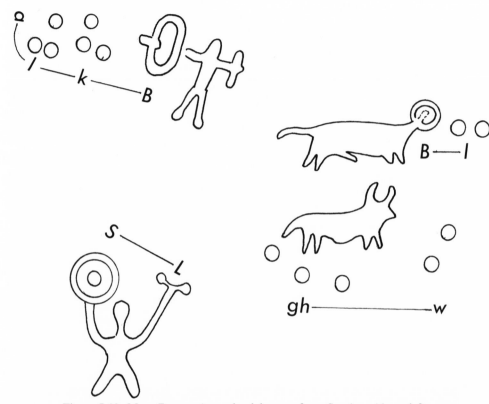

Figure I-10. More Bronze Age school lessons from Sweden. Above left, a man holds a shield, which is drawn to form the Tifinag letter B, so that the inscription reads from right to left as B-K-L-A, Old Norse *bukla*, meaning shield (or buckler). On the right a bull is led to a cow; the bull's head forms the letter B, to yield B-L, Old Norse *beli*, "a bull," and the cow is labeled GH-W, apparently for Old Norse *ku*, the dative case of *kyr*, "a cow." The text is probably to be understood as "a bull for a cow" or "A bull is led to a cow." Lower left, the sun god Sol holds the consonants that spell his name S-L; the letters can also be read from right to left, to yield L-S, Old Norse *lysa*, giving a palindrome that becomes *Sol lysa*, "The sun shines." The first two petrogylphs are from Bohuslän, the third from Östfold.

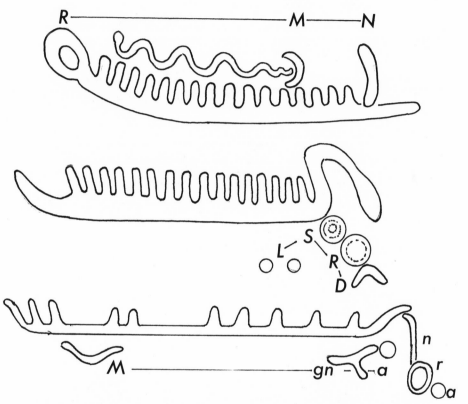

Figure I-11. Three of the named vessels of a Bronze Age fleet depicted in petroglyphs at Lökeberget, Bohuslän. Above, a sixteen-oar ship named R-M-N, Old Norse *Orminn, The Serpent.* Middle, another sixteen-oar ship, whose name in letters reading from right to left is given as D-R-S-L, Old Norse *Drasil, Steed.* Below, a nine-oar support ship named M-GN-A N R-A, Old Norse *Magna ni-aera,* the *Power of Nine Oarsmen.* Nine was a number that imparted magic power.

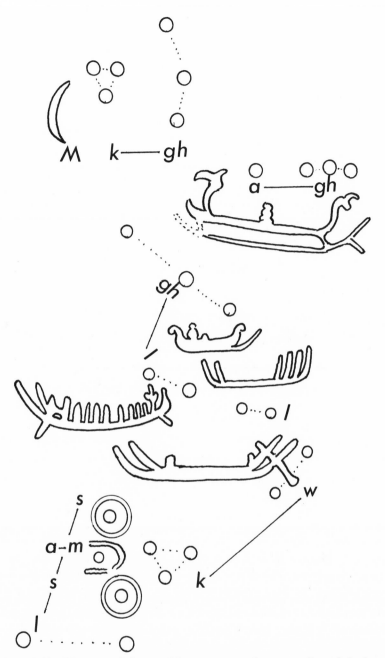

Figure I-12. "May a gentle breeze drive our cogs and may we all reach harbor together." This prayer is engraved at Vanlös, Bohuslän. The text, interwoven among ships, reads as follows: M K-GH A-GH GH-L L W-K S-A-M-S-L, and is probably to be understood as Old Norse *Ma kugge aga gul ol vik samslá*. Some warrior figures were apparently added by another engraver, are unrelated to the text, and have been omitted from the diagram above.

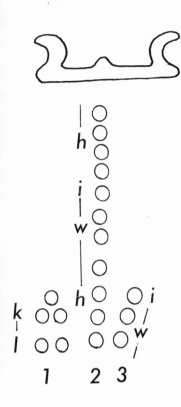

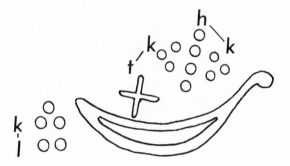

Figure I-13. A fishing charm or prayer from Bohuslän in which the Tifinag letters are arranged to form a rebus depicting a fishing line. One solution may be obtained by reading the letters upward in the sequence shown, to yield L-K H-W-I H-W-I, which may be interpreted as *Lak(s) hafim havim,* "May we haul salmon from the sea." Another solution is obtained by reading the letters in the opposite direction (downward), to yield "May our keeled vessel haul [fish] from the sea." Another similar rebus occurs at Bohuslän, and is shown lower right. It may be read as *lak(s) taka haki,* "May salmon take the hook."

ed—the vessel is called the *Serpent,* and a serpent is shown between the letters that spell the word.

Prayers for Ships at Sea

Figure I-12 shows part of an inscription at Vanlös, Bohuslän, in which a winding strand of Tifinag letters weaves through a series of carvings of Bronze Age ships. The decipherment, as given in the caption, shows that the work was intended as some kind of charm to enable seagoing cogs to remain together, with a fair wind, and to arrive at their destination all at the same time. Figure I-13 shows two charms or prayer inscriptions intended to cause fish to take the hook. The upper illustration has the Tifinag letters laid out in a vertical column; it is a rebus simulating a fishing line with a hook at the lower end. Analogous inscriptions in Celtic dialects commonly form rebus arrangements of ogam letters, so we must conclude that texts of this type were part of the whole Nordic culture during the Bronze Age and were by no means confined to Scandinavia.

Religious Festivals

Figures I-14 to I-17 illustrate a portion of a series of petroglyphs that occur on one rock face at Fossum, Bohuslän, all depicting various aspects of the events that occurred during the celebration of the Thorri festival, held during January and February. Figure I-14 shows the symbol of the festival, a sign made up of reduplicated letters of the name Thorri, resembling a thunderbolt symbol. There follows a scene in which the trumpeters, the lur-blowers, hold these curved instruments to their mouths, and an appropriate text tells us that this began the day's ceremonies. Below, in Figure I-14, we see a scene from what appears to be a hockey game, appropriately labeled "ball game." Dueling with maces is the subject of Figure I-15, the competitors each wearing a sword, all as usual in this period displaying their phalluses. Figure I-16 shows petroglyphs of sorcerers performing feats of juggling, the balls that they throw into the air being the letters of the inscription itself. Figure I-17 depicts hunting with the bow and arrow and an archery contest held in connection with the Thorri festival. Notable in these texts is the use of ship symbols to provide punning words that suggest the actual word intended by the consonants or even that replace spelled-out words. The captions to these figures explain the points of interest.

With these introductory examples, I think it is now appropriate to leave the Swedish scene, where our readers have perhaps some questions to pose to the archaeologists of Stockholm. As for us here in the Americas, we too have matters to settle with our own archaeologists.

But we epigraphers, who study ancient inscriptions, have some explaining to do ourselves. How is it that a Berber alphabet can occur in Scandinavian Bronze Age contexts? Why does a Celtic script also occur there? Why do both scripts (and many others) occur as rock-cut inscriptions in the Americas? These are matters that have been the topic of my earlier books and research papers. A few brief answers may be inserted here, for readers new to the subject.

In regard to ogam, it is easy to demonstrate the untruth of the claim mentioned above that it is a local London invention dating only from the fourth century A.D. If those who make this claim

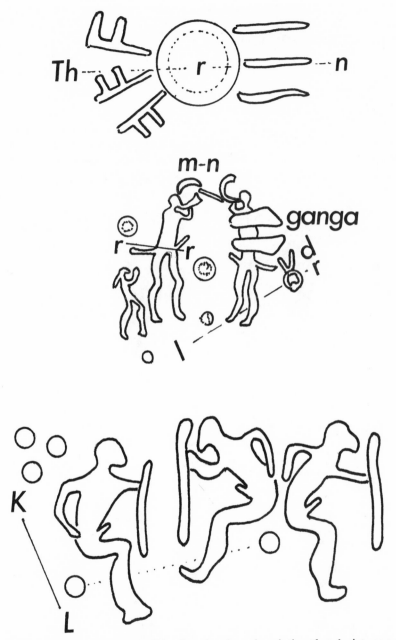

Figure I-14. At Fossum, Bohuslän, there is a large inscription that depicts scenes from the great winter festival called Thorri, held in the fourth month of the Norse six-month winter. These are some of the vignettes. Above, the symbol of Thorri formed from the Tifinag letters *th*, *r* and *n*, repeated and arranged to make a thunderbolt design, Old Norse *Thorinn*, "The Thorri festival." Middle, ceremonies open at dawn when trumpet-blowers summon the people. The Tifinag letters are interwoven with the picture, and the word *ganga* is represented by a punning hieroglyph of footprints, also pronounced as *ganga*. The text reads R-R GANGA L-D-R M-N, to be read as Old Norse *Arar ganga ludramenn*, "early morning the sound of trumpet-blowers." Below, a scene from the hockey or ball game, K-L, Old Norse *kula*, "ball game."

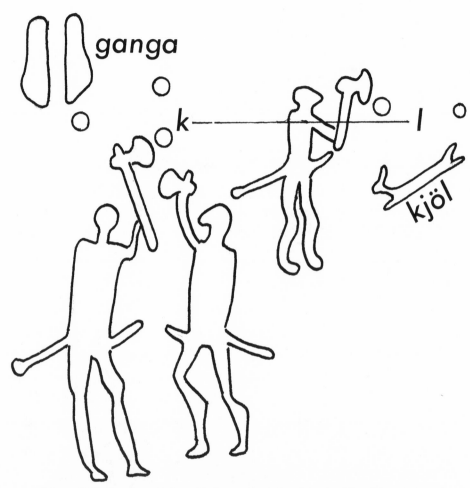

Figure I-15. Another of the athletic events depicted in the Thorri inscription at Fossum, Bohuslän. It may be read as *ganga Kóla*, "fight with maces." The footprint hieroglyph *ganga* (to walk) here represents the same word, but used in the sense of an encounter or fight (*ganga* has numerous meanings in Old Norse). The keeled ship to the right is another punning hieroglyph, in which the word *kjol* approximates the sound of the word for mace or club, *köl*. If the hieroglyph were omitted, the reader would be left in uncertainty as to the included vowel, since only rudimentary vowel signs occur in the Tifinag script.

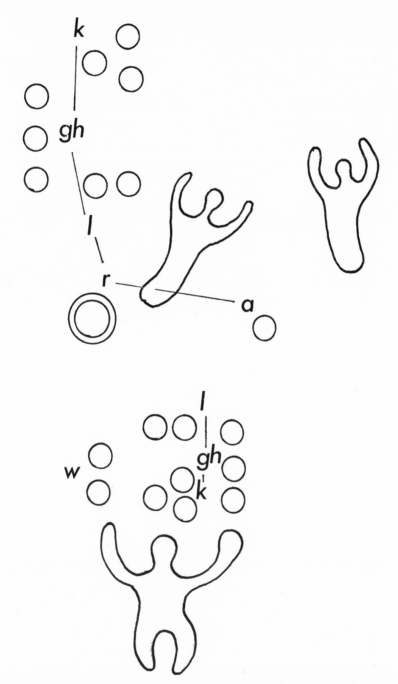

Figure I-16. Sorcery by means of juggling balls was practiced by the ancient Nordic wizards, and the Old Norse word *kuglari* means both "sorcery" and "juggling." The above figures from the Thorri festival inscriptions of Bohuslän show sorcerers. Above, K-GH-L-R-A, Old Norse *kuglari*, "sorcery." Below, W K-GH-L, Old Norse *va kugla*, "He has raised the balls."

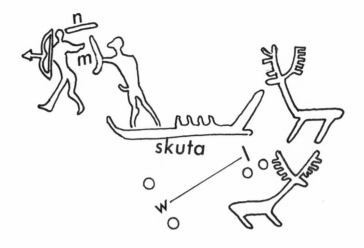

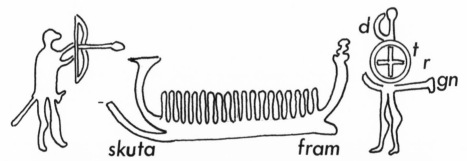

Figure I-17. More vignettes of athletic competition at the Thorri festival, as depicted in the great inscription at Fossum, Bohuslän. The seemingly incongruous ships
are here serving as phonetic punning hieroglyphs (isophones), giving words whose
sound approximates that of the object depicted. The upper inscription is to be read
as M-N SKUTA W-L, Old Norse *menn skjöda villi,* "men shooting wild deer."
The skiff is called *skuta* in Old Norse, close to the sound of the verb *shoot.* In the
lower vignette a large ship appears, and the key isophones here are *skuta,* in this
case meaning "stern," and *fram,* meaning "bow." But *skuta fram* approximates the
sound of *skjöda fram,* "to shoot the farthest." Thus the text reads in Old Norse
skjoda fram ad targinn, "shooting the farthest at the target." The target is a targe,
a round shied held by the partner, whose accouterments form the letters required,
as shown. This sport seems to have been rendered harmless by removing the head
from the arrow or by enclosing the head in wrapping. The antlers of the deer evidently contain a cryptic ogam text, as yet unsolved.

(British archaeologists) should take the time to visit the numismatic department of the British Museum they would see examples of the silver coinage of the Aquitanian Gauls, struck in the second century B.C. and lettered in ogam consaine. They would also see Iberian and Basque imitations of these, lettered in ogam. If they should look at the artifacts excavated from the Windmill Hill site occupied around 2000 B.C. by the builders of Stonehenge, they would see ogam consaine engraved on these, too.

As regards the Tifinag alphabet of the Berbers, a discussion of its origin is given in Chapters 4 and 17. My thesis is that Tifinag is in fact an ancient Nordic script, and that it was taken to North Africa, probably in the twelfth century B.C., when the pharaoh Ramesses III repelled an attack by sea peoples who appear (in his bas-reliefs) to be Norsemen. The invaders took refuge in Libya, and I suspect that the Old Norse runes went with them, and survived as the Tifinag. During my work in North Africa I met Berbers who had no tradition of their origin but who were obviously Europoid, with fair hair, blue, gray, or hazel eyes, and typical European features.

And as for how European skippers could have reached the Americas in the early Bronze Age, I leave their own spokesman, King Woden-lithi himself, to handle that question. He does so in the words he had inscribed on limestone in Canada 3,500 years ago, during the five months he spent in Ontario. And as for why Europe chose to forget about America, that is a matter primarily for European historians to explain, but I would point out that the earth's climate became colder at the end of the Bronze Age, when the north polar icecap came into being. Sailing westward by the northern route became hazardous until the amelioration of climate that took place just before the onset of the Viking period.

Perhaps, when the study of rock inscriptions in Scandinavia is pursued more widely, new evidence may be discovered that could help to fill in some of the missing pieces of the record of man upon the high seas. The increasing frigidity of the North Atlantic as the warm Bronze Age came to an end would not have been the only factor that might have tended to discourage transatlantic trading.

There were also changes occurring in the pattern of commerce in Europe, as the Bronze Age advanced, and these, combined with gradual exhaustion of available upper-level deposits of metallic copper in Canada, probably turned the attention of Scandinavian skippers more to the south and less to the remote lands across the Atlantic.

By 1200 B.C., when the Scandinavian Bronze Age was reaching its peak, traders from the Carthaginian settlements in Spain and Tunisia were reaching the Baltic lands. They brought with them another alphabet, the Iberian, itself a development of the Phoenician way of writing. As is set out in Chapter 14, Scandinavian inscriptions now assume the character of commercial documents, engraved on small pieces of bone, written in the Iberian script, and recording business transactions. It was probably at this epoch that Scandinavian leaders decided that the time had come to discard the old Tifinag letters of King Woden-lithi's day and to modernize their business records by adopting the new Iberian script. So only the religious inscriptions preserved the Tifinag in the northern lands. On the southern shores of the Mediterranean, roving Norse raiders also preserved their Tifinag, which ultimately became the inheritance of the Berber peoples.

The alphabet may not have been the only bequest these Norsemen made to their successors who settled in the Atlas Mountains. When I was working in Libya I noticed among Berbers some words still in use that had a familiar Nordic sound, made even more recognizable now that we can see how King Woden-lithi would have written these same words. Here are some examples. (See Table 1.)

Table 1.

Apparent Old Norse or Old Teutonic Roots in the Berber Language.
(Examples from Ali Sidhi Ahmed et al., *Dictionnaire français-berbère*, Imprimerie Royale, Paris, 1844.) Abbreviations: ON, Old Norse; Dan, Danish; OFaer, Old Faeroese; OE, Old English. Where no mark occurs, as in *men* (= but), the root occurs in all Scandinavian tongues.

The origin of the Tifinag alphabet is discussed in Chapter 4, and the possible reason why it has survived among the North African Berbers is the subject of Chapter 17.

Meaning of word	Scandinavian roots		Berber roots	
	in Latin script	in Tifinag script	in Latin script	in Tifinag script
hale, heal	(ON) heil (Dan) hale	h—l	ahlu	a—h—l
but	men	M—n	men	m—n
eat	(ON) ete	a—t	et, it	a—t
person in authority	(ON) valdr	w—l—d—r	waldin	w—l—d—n
thunder	(ON) Thor (Dan) torden	t—r—d—n	terad	t—r—d
see	(OFaer) siggja	s—gh—ya	sig	s—y—gh
breed, increase	(ON) auka	a—w—k	ek, eg	a—k
means, provisions	(ON) munnr	m—w—n—r	muna	m—w—n—r
meaning, signify	(OE) maenan	m—n—n	mana	m—n
native, born	(ON) aett	a—t	ait	a—t
one	(ON) einn	y—n	yuen	y—w—n
bad, dire	(Dan) dårlig (E) dire	d—r	diri	d—r
bide, stay	(ON) bidhe	b—d	bed	b—d

1

A ROYAL VISITOR—1700 B.C.

Some seventeen centuries before the time of Christ a Nordic king named Woden-lithi sailed across the Atlantic and entered the St. Lawrence River. He reached the neighborhood of where Toronto now stands, and established a trading colony with a religious and commercial center at the place that is now known as Petroglyphs Park, at Peterborough. His homeland was Norway, his capital at Ringerike, west of the head of Oslo Fjord. He remained in Canada for five months, from April to September, trading his cargo of woven material for copper ingots obtained from the local Algonquians (whom he called *Wal,* a word cognate with *Wales* and *Welsh* and meaning "foreigners"). He left behind an inscription that records his visit, his religious beliefs, a standard of measures for cloth and cordage, and an astronomical observatory for determining the Nordic calendar year, which began in March, and for determining the dates of the Yule and pagan Easter festivals. Having provided his colonists with these essentials, he sailed back to Scandinavia and thereafter disappears into the limbo of unwritten Bronze Age history. The king's inscription gives his Scandinavian title only and makes no claim to the discovery of the Americas nor to conquest of territory. Clearly he was not the first visitor to the Americas from Europe, for he found that the Ojibwa Algonquians were already acquainted with the ancient Basque syllabary, and when Woden-lithi set sail for home, an Ojibwa scribe cut a short comment into the rock at the site, using the ancient Basque script and a form of Algonquian still comprehensible today, despite the lapse of time.

The foregoing summary of the findings included in this book calls for an immediate statement about the evidence supporting such sweeping claims.

The primary physical evidence comprises a series of inscriptions cut in the Tifinag and ogam consaine alphabets, using an early form of the Norse tongue, scattered around the outer margins of the petroglyph site at Peterborough (Figures 1-1 and 1-2). Except for the central sun-god and moon-goddess figures and certain astronomical axes cut across the site, the numerous inscriptions are the work of later Algonquian artists, who used King Woden-lithi's inscription as a model for their own, more conspicuous, carvings. The site has been since 1972 under official government protection, and instructions for reaching it are given by the Ontario Ministry of Natural Resources in various guide booklets and pamphlets available to the general public. Readers of this book will find most helpful the ministry's book *Petroglyphs Provincial Park, Master Plan;* also valuable for its treatment of the Algonquian art at the site is the work by Joan M. and Romas K. Vastokas entitled *Sacred Art of the Algonkians* (Mansard Press, 1973). The latter work is meticulous in its accurate portrayal of the inscriptions, in their present eroded state, though the authors did not then recognize the inscribed alphabets or record them as such. The important fact is that professional anthropologists such as the Vastokas team found and recorded the inscriptions and reported that they must date back to a period before the historical occupation of the region by the Hurons and later by Iroquois; in other words, the inscriptions could not be modern features, and must date back to the era of Algonquian occupation, which came to an end some five centuries ago.

Joan and Romas Vastokas recognized apparent Scandinavian and Bronze Age features in the art style. They pointed out that the ships depicted in the inscription are shown in the European manner, with animal figureheads and stern tailpieces, features totally unknown in Algonquian, or indeed in any American Indian, art. They, and other archaeologists, noticed the strange similarities of the central sun-god figure and associated motifs to corresponding solar deities of Europe, especially the Bronze Age petroglyphs of Scandinavia. Other characteristic Scandinavian features that their photographs and drawings record are such elements of Norse my-

Figure 1-1. General view of part of the site near Peterborough, Ontario. Only the more conspicuous markings have been delineated by a black wax crayon applied by site personnel. These stress the large elements added later by Algonquian artists. For the finer Tifinag letters, most of them not marked by crayon, reference should be made to the detailed plan included in *Sacred Art of the Algonkians* by Joan M. and Romas K. Vastokas (Mansard Press, 1973). This photo shows Otto Devitt working at the site, making detailed transparencies to be used in preparing *Bronze Age America*. The area visible includes the central sighting point of the main sun-god figure and part of the east-facing slope. *Photo Russell Tilt.*

Figure 1-2. Detail at Peterborough site, about 20 feet northwest of the main sun figure, showing (above) part of a sea battle, with Tifinag letters marked in black crayon. For a decipherment see Figure I-7. *Photo Otto Devitt.*

thology as the maiming of the god of war by the Fenrir wolf (Chapters 9 and 13 of this book), the conspicuous short-handled hammer, Mjolnir, of Thunor (Thor of the Norse), and Gungnir, the spear of Woden (Chapters 7 and 10 of this book), both of which were imitated many times over by the Algonquian artists who later occupied the site. Thus the purely objective reports made by the Vastokases, who sought only to record what they discovered, without attaching any interpretation other than that appropriate for Algonquian art, have an added value and importance for us now, for they observed the material as it was uncovered from the soil and placed it on permanent record in their photographs, charts, and descriptions. As a result of the initial discoveries, the whole site was set aside as a public park and protected by an enclosure.

Thus, the primary evidence still exists and is open for public inspection under circumstances that prevent the possible vandalization of the site. The only disturbing feature is that, since the inscriptions were exposed to the air, after removal of the covering soil that had protected them, the action of frost and acid rain has caused a gradual deterioration of the surface of the limestone. Unless steps are taken to impregnate the bedrock with a stabilizer, such as silicone, the precious record may soon melt away into unreadable markings, as part indeed already had before the site had been found.

The actual discovery should be noted here. It occurred on May 12, 1954, and was made by three geologists, Ernest Craig, Charles Phipps, and Everitt Davis, in the course of fieldwork on mining claims. The following day "Nick" Nickels, a photographer-journalist of the *Peterborough Examiner,* visited the site, and so began the first modern records of it. Paul Sweetman of the University of Toronto undertook the first research at the site in July 1954, recording nearly a hundred petroglyphs. Sweetman's report indicated a possible age as great as 3,500 years or as young as 400 years. His upper limit, 3,500 years, is in agreement with the epigraphic evidence as given in this book. Tens of thousands of visitors now come to the site each year, using the access road and other facilities that have been erected for their benefit. It has become a major center of archaeological interest for the whole of North America, and all Americans are grateful to the Canadian authorities for having seen to it that the ancient petroglyphs are protected yet open to all visitors.

The Vastokases, like most archaeologists in North America, felt obliged to explain all American petroglyphs as being the work of native Amerindian artists. Despite their, and others', perception of the similarities to Scandinavian petroglyphs of the Bronze Age, the idea that any connection might have existed between North America and Scandinavia in the Bronze Age, some 3,500 years ago, seemed preposterous. So they were faced with remarkable parallels, yet they elected to explain them as no more than chance similarities brought about by a shamanistic view of the sky as a kind of sea on which the sun and the moon sailed their ships to cross the heavens each day.

In treating the inscriptions in this way, they were following the example of other distinguished anthropologists and archaeologists who had investigated North American petroglyphs. The leading researcher during the last several decades had been Professor Robert Heizer of the University of California. He was vehement in his rejection of all theories that America had been visited in pre-Columbian times by voyagers from Europe, Africa, or elsewhere, and he chose to view all American petroglyphs as the products of Amerindians. He did take account of age-determination techniques, such as those dependent on carbon-dating of materials found in caves where petroglyphs occur and the evidence provided by the oxidation of rocks, especially in dry climates such as eastern California, Nevada, and Arizona. These methods enabled Heizer to set dates of up to five thousand years ago for some petroglyphs. As for me, at the time when the Ontario petroglyphs were discovered, I had just completed a comprehensive Scandinavian journey and had visited many of the famous inscriptions of Sweden and Denmark, though I was still a long way from recognizing the Tifinag alphabet at any Bronze Age petroglyph site beyond the shores of North Africa.

My subsequent work on Tifinag led to the gradual decipherment of the ancient language of Libya and, after various Libyan scholars visited me at Harvard, I was invited to lecture on the Tifinag inscriptions at the universities of Tripoli and Benghazi. Just before leaving for North Africa in 1977, I had received from Otto Devitt the first of what were to be a continuing series of photographs he made for me of the petroglyphs at Peterborough. Although I could see that the site included Tifinag letters, the words

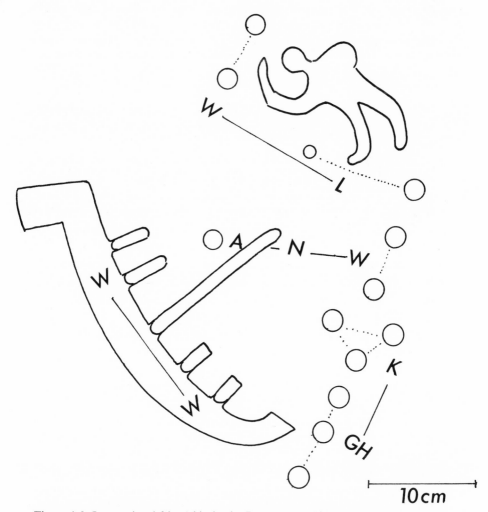

Figure 1-3. International friendship in the Bronze Age. This cunningly composed Norse rebus in Tifinag script lies 14 feet southeast-by-east of the main sun-god figure. It reads "Wal wina wawa kogha" (Old Norse *Val vinnr vafa kogga*, "A foreign friend waves to the ship"). The foreign friend would be an Algonquian Indian, probably of the Ojibwa tribe, who were trading copper ingots from the Lake Superior mines for cloth from Scandinavian looms. The inscription can be read, with the same meaning, if it be taken as a dialect of Anglo-Saxon. *Peterborough Provincial Park, Ontario.*

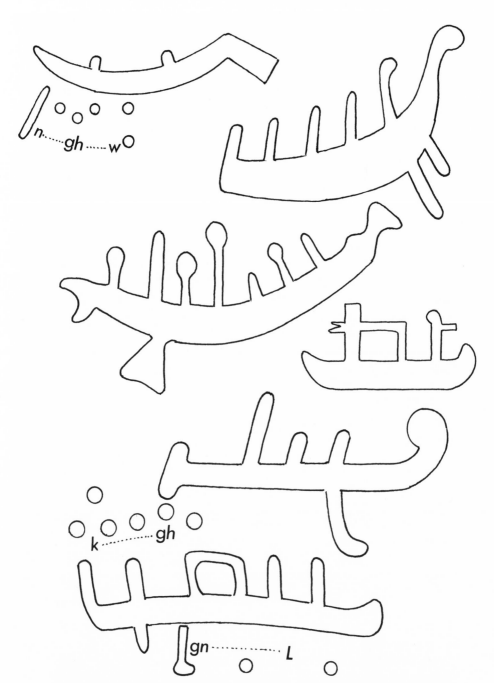

Figure 1-4. Some of the vessels depicted by King Woden-lithi's artists at Peterborough, Ontario. Types identified by the scribes include cogs (k-gh), longships (L-gn), and *Nokve* (n-gh-w).

they formed seemed to have no discernible connection with the language of ancient Libya, and I was forced to put the slides aside while I undertook other assignments.

In the interim I read some of Heizer's reports on the petroglyphs of eastern California and Nevada, and recognized that they included Tifinag and Kufi (early Arabic). A particularly striking case is the petroglyph in Owens Valley, California, that depicts the entire zodiac, in the form it had before the third century B.C., together with a Kufi inscription explaining that the new year is determined at the time of the vernal equinox, when the sun enters the constellation of the Ram. One of my former Harvard students, Dr. Jon Polansky, was now doing research at Berkeley, and he made the acquaintance of Professor Heizer and showed him the decipherment I had done on his Owens Valley petroglyphs. As a consequence Professor Heizer invited me to visit him; this came about in May 1979. We became friends and, putting aside his former opposition to the notion of pre-Columbian visitors, Bob Heizer now carefully checked each element of the decipherment and confirmed that I had rendered his original published diagrams correctly in the version in which I inserted the sound values of the Kufi signs. We planned a joint publication, but illness prevented him from accompanying me into the desert that year. Instead, he arranged for one of his former Berkeley students, Dr. Christopher Corson, to take me to some of the inscription areas. Dr. Corson, an archaeologist in the Bureau of Land Management, has the best knowledge of petroglyph sites in northern California and northwest Nevada. He led a party that included John Williams, Jon Polansky, and me, together with Wayne and Betty Struble and their son Peter. Bob Heizer planned to take part in my next field trip, but to our great regret he passed away, struck down by the illness that had already prevented his participation in the 1979 fieldwork. I was obliged to publish the Owens Valley zodiac without the benefit of his contribution, though the illustrations of the paper had been checked by him for accuracy and had his approval.

Dr. Heizer's contribution to American petroglyph studies has been immense, and my colleagues and I knew that a significant point had been reached when Heizer recognized the true nature of the Owens Valley zodiac and opened his mind to a new view of

American prehistory in which pre-Columbian visitors and colonists would now play a role. Heizer, as archaeologist and anthropologist, filled an intermediate position between those archaeologists who devote their research to excavation of ancient sites and epigraphers, those linguists who give their energies to the decipherment of ancient inscriptions.

By 1979, the same season in which Heizer and I had begun to influence each other, the epigraphers of Europe had already begun to analyze my work on ancient inscriptions in America, and soon authoritative publications began to appear, giving strong support and confirmation. Professor Pennar Davies, a leading Welsh scholar, and, in America, Professor Sanford Etheridge, editor of *Gaeltacht* (an Irish-language publication), had both written in support of my finding ogam inscriptions in America. In Spain, the leading Basque scholar, Dr. Imanol Agiŕe, advised me that he too confirmed my reports on Basque inscriptions in Pennsylvania, dating from about the ninth century before Christ. In 1980 the volume he contributed to the *Gran Enciclopedia Vasca* (Great Basque Encyclopedia) contained letter-by-letter analyses of my papers, and in a technical paper published in 1981 Agiŕe acknowledged that my decipherment of the ancient Basque syllabary is correct. These and other published papers, such as those of the Swiss linguist Professor Linus Brunner, provided competent scholarly approval of our American studies on the alphabets and syllabaries that are represented at the site in Peterborough. Their opinions, therefore, together with the detailed analyses that they have published, must be taken into account when some archaeologists, both in America and Britain, attempt to discredit the research on American inscriptions. The claims of the latter that epigraphers in America are deluded by forgeries, or even forge the alleged inscriptions themselves, have to be dismissed as ignorant remarks made without personal knowledge of the scripts or the languages involved, and generally without any knowledge of the sites at which the inscriptions occur.

From the information I have given in this chapter it is obvious that the petroglyphs at Peterborough cannot be forgeries, and that they are ancient. From the information given in the previous chapter and those that follow, it is easy for any person who so de-

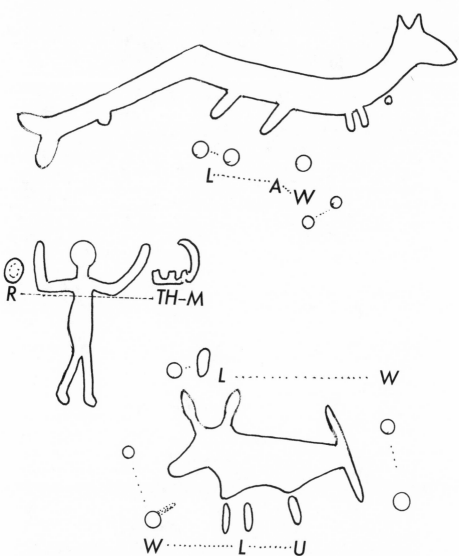

Figure 1-5. What the visitors saw in America. W-A-L (Old Norse *hval*, whale); M-TH-R (Old Norse *Madhr* man, an Algonquian); W-L U-L-W (Old Norse *val ulf*, foreign—i.e., American—wolf). The whale lies 18 feet southwest of the main sun-god figure; the man is immediately to the left of the sun god, the wolf 12 feet to the southwest of the sun god. These examples all use retrograde writing direction. The wolf is a rebus, hence the legs are shown separated from the body.

sires to check the statements and conclusions, and, as in previous books I have written, I invite them to do so. Only by such methods can we eventually persuade Americans to realize that American history extends far into the past, and that America and Europe interacted through trade and cultural contact for over three thousand years before Columbus made his first voyage.

Since my first book on ancient voyages to America, some important advances have been made in archaeological research bearing on that topic. In New England James P. Whittall and members of the Early Sites Research Society have discovered and excavated a site (a disk barrow) that was first occupied seven thousand years ago. Some of the skeletons show the characteristics of Europeans, yet their age by carbon-dating is at least 1,600 years. One of the skulls matches closely the skulls of the ancient Irish. These facts have been determined by an anthropologist, Professor Albert Casey, whose research has been devoted to skull and bone characteristics of Old World peoples. His computer is programmed to recognize Old World characteristics in New World skulls now being discovered. The tumuli of northeastern America show great similarities to those of Europe. The radiocarbon dates indicate similar ranges in time. The artifacts excavated from American burial sites, sometimes in actual contact with the skeletons of their presumed former owners, have been discovered in some cases to have inscriptions carved upon them, in ogam and Basque script; to Dr. William P. Grigsby we owe this observation, based on his own extensive collections of artifacts from the southeastern states.

We are faced, therefore, with what amounts to conclusive evidence that the artifacts (including written inscriptions) of European peoples of the Bronze Age are found at American archaeological sites, and with these artifacts skeletons are occasionally found that conform to Europoid criteria. The recognition and confirmation of the inscriptions are due to epigraphers who have published their findings and who, in most cases, teach courses in linguistics or epigraphy at reputable universities. Thus, whether or not we can comprehend the sailing techniques of Bronze Age peoples, the fact seems inescapable that Bronze Age Europeans reached North America. My personal view is that the mild climate of the Bronze Age permitted navigation to take advantage of the westward-flow-

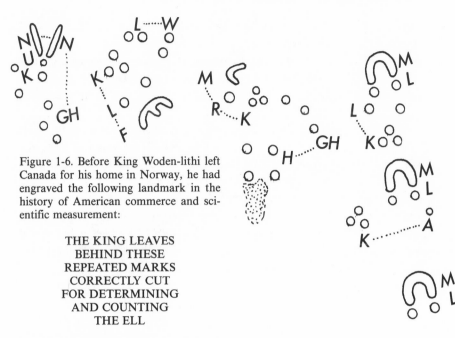

Figure 1-6. Before King Woden-lithi left Canada for his home in Norway, he had engraved the following landmark in the history of American commerce and scientific measurement:

THE KING LEAVES
BEHIND THESE
REPEATED MARKS
CORRECTLY CUT
FOR DETERMINING
AND COUNTING
THE ELL

It lies 18 feet east of the sun god. The Scandinavian *alen*, or ell, was a unit of length, the length of the forearm (Old Norse *oln*) from the elbow to the tip of the middle finger; it was approximately 18 inches in span, varying a little from one country to another. These marks are the oldest known standard of measurement for any Nordic land. In later ages the ell came to signify about 45 inches. The words in the inscription are:

M-L (*mal* = measurement)
K-U-N-N-GH (*Konungr* = King)
L-W (*lav* = leave behind)
K-L-F (*klifa* = repeated)
M-R-K (*merki* = marks)
L-K (*laki* = correct position)
A-K (*aka* = determine)
R-GN (*regna* = to reckon)
L-N (*aln, oln* = the ell, ca 18")
H-GH (*hugga* = cut, hack)

This clearly legible text is the most ancient example of a written language lying directly in the ancestry of English.

ing currents and westward-blowing winds of the polar regions, and thus made the natural northern route to North America much easier to use than is the case today, when polar ice intrudes and savage weather occurs. I have sailed that route and appreciate its discomforts. They would have been much less severe in the Bronze Age, while the attraction of North America for Scandinavian skippers would have been much enhanced by the availability of copper in metallic form, at a time when Europe was demanding copper for bronze alloys on a larger scale than ever before or since. These matters are treated in more detail in later chapters; they are given here merely to provide a rounded introduction to the subject.

Before entering into a more detailed discussion of King Woden-lithi's mission in North America, it would be useful to review the salient features of the northern world at the era when he lived, in the early part of the Bronze Age.

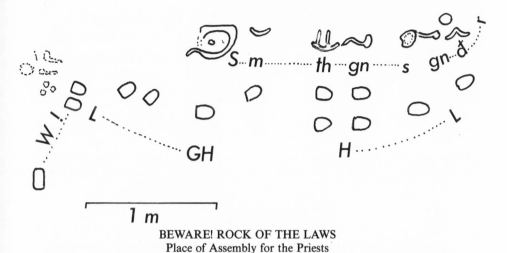

BEWARE! ROCK OF THE LAWS
Place of Assembly for the Priests

Figure 1-7. So reads the ancient public notice engraved in 12-inch Tifinag letters at the northeastern extremity of the Peterborough site, evidently the original point of entry. The letters are consonants only, yet their concatenation is an astonishing repetition of the technical legal terms known to have been used in Iceland in Viking times, some 2,000 years after King Woden-lithi. In Iceland, too, in pagan times there was an annual assembly of the priests; it was called *Samthingis-Godhar.* In Woden-lithi's dialect of ancient Nordic speech there was more aspiration: *g* was *gh*, and *ng* was *gn*; *d* was apparently always pronounced as *dh*; i.e., the sound of *th* in the English word *this*.

In ancient Iceland, as in ancient Scandinavia, there was an annual meeting of the pagan priests at which the laws were declaimed by a law-speaker. The place at which this ceremony was held was called the *Lög-Berg,* or Hill of the Law. Here in America, at Peterborough, the site selected was a flat rock platform. The ancient Norse word *hella* means a flat rock; evidently, therefore, the ancient name of the Peterborough site was *Lögh-Hella,* which could be pronounced by English speakers today roughly as if it were spelled "Lurg-hella."

2
A VIEW OF THE BRONZE AGE

In northern Europe bronze weapons and implements first began to replace the stone artifacts of the Neolithic inhabitants when trade routes to the Mediterranean lands permitted imports from the south. The change from stone and malleable copper to the more durable and more valuable bronze equipment is dated to about 2000 B.C.

At this time, which marks the opening of the Bronze Age, the most numerous and conspicuous man-made features of the landscape were the massive drystone monuments that had been erected during the last phases of the Neolithic, from about 2200 B.C. onward. These great monuments, called *megaliths* (from Greek roots meaning *huge stones*) have remained an impressive feature of the European landscape ever since, and today tens of thousands of tourists visit the megalithic sites every year, to gaze with wonder at these mysterious works of our ancestors.

When the English Pilgrims began to settle northeastern North America in the early 1600s they found that the forests and open hillsides carried similar ancient stone monuments. Governor John Winthrop (the Younger) of Connecticut had become during his student years one of the first Fellows of the infant Royal Society, and after his arrival in America was regarded by the colonists as a fount of information on all matters to do with natural history and antiquities. He wrote papers for the early volumes of the *Philosophical Transactions* (published by the Royal Society in London) and thus drew attention to the salient features of scientific interest in his new world across the Atlantic. Among his papers is found evidence of inquiries from settlers as to what could be the meaning of the strange stone "forts" they were encountering. It was noted that the Algonquian Indians did not use stone in their constructions (save for some rare instances), and the Indians themselves shunned the stone chambers and could throw no light on their origins.

Toward the close of the nineteenth century the opinions of a few influential archaeologists in North America were that no European had set foot in America until the time of Columbus. Since such opinions precluded any possibility that the stone monuments of New England might be related to the megalithic monuments of Europe, the entire subject fell out of favor. Americans were sent to Europe to study Stone Age and Bronze Age archaeology, and few, if any, thought to pay attention to the problems raised by the New England megaliths. So deeply ingrained is this view of the agelong isolation of America that when in 1976 I published my reasoned thoughts on the parallels between American and European archaeological sites, my book *America B.C.* was dismissed by most archaeologists as ignorant rubbish. In reality, much of my reasoning was based on a careful comparison of engraved inscriptions found on the associated stonework, both in European sites (especially Portugal and Spain) and in American contexts. I recorded, for example, well-known Iberian scripts of the late Bronze Age, found on hundreds of rocks in Pennsylvania, and my decipherments, utilizing Professor David Diringer's tables in *The Alphabet* (Hutchinson, 1968). Such works as Resurrección María de Azukue's *Diccionario Vasco-Español-Frances* (Bilbao, 1969) enabled me to recognize and report Basque gravestones and boundary marker stones, apparently dating from about the era of 900 B.C.

European epigraphers and linguists, such as the foremost Basque scholars, carried out detailed checks on my findings, confirmed most of them, and, as I have said, in the latest volume of the *Gran Enciclopedia Vasca* several chapters are now given over to matters raised by these American Basque inscriptions, and the analysis by Imanol Agíre in his *Vínculos de la lengua vasca* gives a virtual total confirmation of my findings: the inscriptions, in Agíre's opinion, do date from about 900 B.C. and they do carry Basque phrases in the appropriate Iberian alphabets of that period. These findings have been the object of much discussion by archaeologists. For a current summary of the subject, reference may be made to the *Occasional Publications* of the Epigraphic Society, volume 9 (1981), where some fifty opinions, pro and con, are set out. In general, it can be said in summary that linguists and epigraphers agree that the American inscriptions are genuine and ancient, and that many of them relate to the Bronze Age.

Since linguists and epigraphers concur that the American inscriptions do include genuine products of Bronze Age scribes, and that the scripts and languages used show that the scribes came from European and North African lands, there is no longer any basis for doubting that the monuments of North America that resemble megaliths are indeed just that—megaliths. By this I mean monuments produced by colonists from Europe in Bronze Age times.

Now, a popular book is not the proper place to review the tedious details of various scripts and various languages employed and inscribed by these visitors, who came from so many different lands. Besides, I have already written about these matters in *America B.C.* and *Saga America,* as well as in a round hundred or so technical papers. The most entertaining and attractive entrance to the subject is through visiting some of the sites where American megalithic monuments can be seen, and also through visiting the corresponding sites in Europe where, of course, there is no dispute at all as to the authorship or antiquity of megaliths.

Visual presentation rather than written descriptions forms the best introduction to the monuments, and in the atlas of photographs that I present here, European and American examples of each of the major categories of megaliths are arranged in comparable groups of similar structures.

Radiocarbon and amino-acid dating has only recently been applied to the determination of dates of American megaliths, but analogous features suggesting early European penetration into North America include the low circular burial mounds that are called *disk barrows.* I have mentioned above the investigation of one of these, presently under way in New England by James Whittall. It has so far been learned that Whittall's site was under continuous occupation, at least for ceremonial purposes, from about 5000 B.C. (amino-acid date 7200 Before Present), until about 500 B.C. Over that span of time a number of burials occurred and, as noted in Chapter 1, these include a Europoid skeleton. Associated stone artifacts resemble tools of the era called *Archaic* in America (8000 to 500 B.C.), corresponding to the entire span of the Neolithic and Bronze Age in Europe. Sometime before A.D. 900 a stonework structure was added around the margins of the barrow. These findings by Whittall point strongly to European arrivals in North America long before Bronze Age times.

Other radiocarbon dates show that some of the megalithic chambers in New England are of later date, one in Vermont, for example, yielding charcoal from the foundation layer that gave a carbon date of about A.D. 200.

As for those megalithic monuments that contain no artifacts or charcoal, dates can only be guessed at from indirect evidence. The guesses made in that way suggest that most of them were probably built during Bronze Age and Iron Age times, as indeed many of the European megaliths can be shown to postdate the Neolithic period also. So massive and enduring are megaliths that, whenever they were built, they affected the living space of later peoples, and certainly Bronze Age Europeans utilized the Neolithic megaliths. More detailed information on what the burials disclose is given in two subsequent chapters (Chapter 3 deals with the skeletons, Chapter 13 with the evidence afforded by the associated grave goods). In this chapter I will restrict further comments to the actual megalithic monuments, merely noting here that the disk barrow, with its contained female skeletons lying in flexed positions, is regarded in Europe as a feature of the early Bronze Age and that therefore it is relevant to note here that similar features occur in New England in districts where megalithic monuments occur. My own opinion, of course, remains unaltered; it is that the megalithic monuments of northeastern North America were used during the Bronze Age and therefore may have been constructed either shortly before or during the Bronze Age.

The term *dolmen* is a Breton word meaning a stone table. It aptly describes many of the smaller examples of the megalithic monuments that go under this name. Such smaller examples, a meter or less in height, are shown in Figures 2-1 to 2-6. As can be seen, they comprise an upper, horizontal slab of stone, the *capstone,*

Figure 2-1. Cromlech or funerary dolmen at Carrazeda, Portugal. Formerly buried under earth, the stone structural elements now stand exposed through long-continued weathering. *Photo Leonel Ribeiro.*

Figure 2-2. Exposed cromlech dolmen, Orkney Islands. *Photo Alban Wall.*

Figure 2-3. Cromlech dolmen, Gay Head, Martha's Vineyard, Massachusetts. *Photo William J. Hall.*

Figure 2-4. Small dolmen, Westport, Massachusetts. *Photo James P. Whittall.*

Figure 2-5. Small dolmen, Westport, Massachusetts. *Photo James P. Whittall.*

Figure 2-6. Small dolmen, Hampton, Massachusetts. *Photo James P. Whittall.*

Figure 2-7. John Williams pointing to inscription area at one end-face of the capstone of a collapsed dolmen, central Vermont. *Photo Joseph D. Germano.*

which is supported on several vertical slabs, like a table, with an internal cavity. European archaeologists believe that the central cavity originally contained a burial and that the entire structure was originally buried in earth that has subsequently disappeared through erosion. It is known that some examples had partial earth cover still intact a century or so ago. Such bared burial chambers are often distinguished from other dolmens under the name *cromlech.*

Of the examples shown, Figures 2-1 and 2-2 are European, 2-1 from Carrazeda, Portugal, and 2-2 from the Orkney Islands. The remaining four examples are all American. Figure 2-3 shows an example at Gay Head, on the island of Martha's Vineyard, Massachusetts; a faintly visible ogam inscription occurs on one of the stones at the entrance to the small chamber within (see the Glossary for such words as *ogam,* whose definition would be out of place in this chapter). The others, Figures 2-4, 2-5, and 2-6, are all located at Westport, Massachusetts. Similar ones occur in the Boston area. Nothing is known of any former burial relics in these small cromlechs.

Very much larger examples, with massive capstones and relatively shorter vertical supports, form conspicuous dolmens. These seem unlikely to have been covered by earth at any stage.

Figure 2-7 shows a collapsed dolmen found in Vermont. The finder, John Williams, points to a remarkable sculpted ax and halberd that are cut into one end of the squared capstone (detail in Figure 2-8). A similar occurrence has been reported from an early Bronze Age burial cairn at Nether Largie North, in Scotland, ax heads being engraved on one end of the capstone and a halberd with streamers on another upright stone of the same burial cist. It is difficult to conceive of any Amerindian carving such devices and, as stated, the Algonquians of the New England region have no knowledge of the authors of these stone monuments.

The example from Scotland cited above postdates the Neolithic period, to which megaliths are customarily assigned, and suggests that dolmens are not restricted to a single period. Still more striking evidence is seen in examples from France, such as the one shown in Figure 2-9. The elaborately carved Tuscan columns that serve as the supports for the massive capstone indicate that this dol-

Figure 2-8. Inscribed halberd and, crossed with it, what appears to be a palmleaf, engraved on the capstone of the dolmen shown in the preceding illustration. Similar inscribed details occur on an early Bronze Age dolmen at Nether Largie North, Scotland. *Photo Joseph D. Germano.*

Figure 2-9. Dolmen constructed during or after Classical times in France, with Tuscan columns supporting the partially shaped capstone. Dated Roman coins found under such dolmens attest to their use long after the period in which megaliths were first constructed. *Joseph Dechellette.*

men cannot antedate the Roman era. Also, dated Roman coins have been found under dolmens in France, and other evidence proves that they served as sites for some kind of ceremony even as late as the Middle Ages, when the church authorities regarded such assemblies as the practice of witchcraft. By analogy, then, there are no grounds for insisting that dolmens are restricted to the archaeology of the Neolithic period, as do some British authorities.

The largest of the dolmens utilize natural boulders, sometimes weighing up to 90 tons, supported precariously, so it would seem, on the underlying peg stones, yet their duration through 4,000 years shows their builders to have had a fine sense of stable construction. An example is depicted in Figure 2-10, from Ireland, and another in Trelleborg, Sweden, is shown in Figure 2-11. Corresponding examples from North America are illustrated in Figures 2-12 to 2-16. Figure 2-12 shows the dolmen at Lynn, Massachusetts, locally known as the Cannon Stone. Figure 2-13 is an example from near Lake Lujenda, northern Minnesota, discovered recently by David Harvey, and the first to be reported from that state. The other examples are from Bartlett, New Hampshire (Figure 2-14), and North Salem, New York (Figures 2-15, 2-16).

I find it difficult to distinguish the North American examples from the European ones and believe that both sets were produced by ancient builders who shared a common culture. When the evidence of inscriptions is taken into account, as in later chapters of this book, the relationship of the American examples to those of northern Europe becomes undeniable.

A second category of megaliths is supplied by the underground stone chambers, and on some of these, too, the American ones included, inscriptions are found that use European scripts appropriate to the Bronze Age, as well as later graffiti, which have no bearing on the date of construction. They fall in several categories, according to the mode of construction. Some are in the form of rectangular chambers, up to twenty feet in length by ten feet in width, often with the long axis pointed toward the sunrise direction for either the equinoxes or for one of the solstices. One at Danbury, Connecticut, carries engraved on a fallen lintel stone the ancient symbol of the equinox, a circle divided into equal halves, one half deeply engraved to represent night, the other left clearly visible; this cham-

Figure 2-10. Dolmen of Proleek, County Louth, Ireland. *Norman Totten.*

Figure 2-11. Dolmen with massive capstone, Trelleborg, Sweden. *Photo Joseph D. Germano.*

Figure 2-12. Dolmen with massive (40-ton) capstone at Lynn, Massachusetts. *Photo James P. Whittall.*

Figure 2-13. Newly discovered dolmen at Lake Lujenda, northern Minnesota. *Photo David Harvey.*

Figure 2-14. View of supporting stones of massive capstone of the dolmen at Bartlett, New Hampshire. *Photo John H. Bradner.*

Figure 2-15. The largest known dolmen in North America, with a 90-ton capstone, located at North Salem, New York, and mistakenly attributed by an adjacent sign-post to "the action of the Ice Age." *Photo Renee Fell.*

Figure 2-16. End aspect of the North Salem dolmen, New York. *Photo Renee Fell.*

ber, as John Williams and his colleagues proved, faces the sunrise on the equinox days: that is, it is oriented due east and points to a notch on the horizon within which the sun appears on the days of the vernal and autumnal equinox.

It has been supposed that religious ceremonies were held in the chambers on the day for which the chamber was designed to yield the required sunrise view, and that these ceremonies would also be related to the determination of the start of the new year, at the vernal equinox.

The mode of construction follows patterns appropriate to the type of stone naturally available. Where large slabs can be obtained, these are used as capstones to form the roofing, as in the Danish chambers called *Jaettestuer* ("giants' salons"). Figure 2-17 shows an example at Aarhus, Denmark. North American examples include a large chamber at South Woodstock, Vermont (Figure 2-18). The entrances commonly have a massive lintel stone supported on either two vertical slabs (called orthostats), as in Figure 2-19 (Mystery Hill, North Salem, New Hampshire) or on a drystone vertical column of slabs on either side (Figure 2-20, Mystery Hill). Alternatively, the construction may utilize natural features of the environment, as at Concord, Massachusetts (Figure 2-21), and at Gungywamp, near Groton, Connecticut (Figure 2-22). The chamber may be wholly subterranean, as in one of the White River examples in Vermont (Figure 2-23), or may stand free, as at Mystery Hill (Figure 2-20). In the latter case the details of the wall construction are visible externally (Figure 2-24, Vermont) as drystone and internally (Figure 2-25, Mystery Hill), the latter example showing some degree of trimming of the blocks. The internal chamber is usually rectangular (Figure 2-26, South Woodstock, Vermont), but exceptionally, as in Figure 2-25, the chamber may have lateral passages. Some chambers are covered by mounds, as in the example shown in Figure 2-27, South Woodstock. Where large capstones are not available locally, corbeling is utilized to produce a roofing, as in the chamber at Upton, Massachusetts (Figure 2-28). Chambers of the latter type seem to be related to the similar constructions called *fougou* in Cornwall, England, believed to date from the Iron Age and to have been used in and after Roman times. The function of a fougou is unknown, but food storage or places of refuge are considered

Figure 2-17. Megalithic chamber, or *Jaettestue*, near Aarhus, Denmark. *Photo Joseph D. Germano.*

Figure 2-18. Massive roof lintels of megalithic chamber near South Woodstock, Vermont. *Photo Peter J. Garfall.*

Figure 2-19. Massive orthostats of chamber at Mystery Hill, North Salem, New Hampshire. *Photo Peter J. Garfall.*

Figure 2-20. Slab lintel supported on drystone columns, Mystery Hill, North Salem, New Hampshire. *Photo Peter J. Garfall.*

Figure 2-21. Entrance to subterranean chamber at Concord, Massachusetts. *Photo Renee Fell.*

Figure 2-22. Chamber entrance, utilizing natural features, Gungywamp, near Groton, Connecticut. *Photo Sentiel Rommel.*

Figure 2-23. Emerging from entrance blocked by earth slide, chamber near White River, central Vermont. *Photo Peter J. Garfall.*

Figure 2-24. Free-standing drystone walls, central Vermont. *Photo Joseph D. Germano.*

Figure 2-25. Megalithic construction of internal walls by drystone fitted blocks, Mystery Hill, North Salem, New Hampshire. *Photo Peter J. Garfall.*

Figure 2-26. Rectangular form of internal plan of megalithic chamber, South Woodstock, Vermont. *Photo Peter J. Garfall.*

Figure 2-27. Chamber covered by earth mound, South Woodstock, Vermont. *Photo Byron Dix.*

Figure 2-28. Corbeling construction of the Upton chamber, Massachusetts. *Photo Malcolm Pearson*.

possibilities. The New England tradition is that these chambers were built by the colonists as "root cellars," for storing vegetables. But inquiries disclose that they were already present on some sites at the time of the arrival of the colonists, who, in any case, found that root vegetables survive the winter frost well when buried in straw in the soil, but tend to decay from mold if placed in the so-called root cellars. The enormous labor of construction, as opposed to the simplicity of building a log cabin, denies another legend, that the colonists built the chambers to live in while they were constructing their first farmhouses. Chambers are also found on mountainsides where no farm has ever existed but where a good astronomical viewpoint is obtained.

Like the dolmens, megalithic buildings continued to be utilized, and also to be constructed, until Roman times. Figures 2-29 and 2-30 depict Pictish *broch* construction at Baile Chladaich, northwestern Scotland. The brochs are believed to be defensive structures made around 100 B.C.

Some other distinctive megaliths occur in both Europe and North America. These include phallic monuments of standing stones, called also *dall* or *menhir*. These are noted in Chapter 11 on account of their association with the gods of male fertility. So also the megaliths called *men-a-tol* (Cornish "Hole in the stone") or just "holey-stones," are mentioned in Chapter 14, in connection with the fertility goddesses. The well-known stone rings and monuments such as Stonehenge are also a feature of the megalithic industry. These are mentioned in Chapter 5 in the context of astronomical observatories and calendar regulation. For, although the English archaeologist Glyn Daniel denies any connection of these structures with astronomy, competent astronomers, notably the Thoms, father and son, of the Department of Astronomy, Edinburgh University, and Gerald Hawkins, Fred Hoyle, and John Carlson in America have all concluded that an intimate connection exists between these ring structures and the development of astronomical science.

Figure 2-29. Double wall construction with internal chambers and passages in a Pictish broch, Baile-Chladaich, Sutherland, Scotland. *Photo Barry Fell.*

Figure 2-30. Megalithic construction of Pictish broch, ca. 100 B.C., in Baile Chladaich, Scotland. *Photo Barry Fell.*

3
WHAT THE EXCAVATIONS REVEAL

My professional work as an oceanographer had taken me to various remote oceanic islands, and while there I had learned of the existence of unexplained inscriptions cut in caves or painted in rock shelters. These raised questions as to who had made the inscriptions, and when they had been made. My first paper on Polynesian rock art had appeared under the aegis of the Royal Anthropological Institute in 1941. My colleagues began to look out for inscriptions, too, when they knew of my interest, and I gradually assembled a considerable collection of photographs and .casts as the years went by. I soon became convinced that Stone Age man was by no means an ignorant, land-tied savage. On the contrary, he appeared to me to have been a resourceful and accomplished mariner, who could cross ocean gaps between Pacific islands greater than the total span of the Atlantic Ocean.

As oceanography advanced, methods were developed of sending various ingenious devices down to the ocean floor to take samples by boring into the muds on the bottom. Since mud accumulates extremely slowly far away from the effluence of rivers, even just an inch deep in the ocean floor takes us back to a time of deposition of the mud that amounts to thousands of years. Also, since bones and shells of marine animals fall to the bottom, they are preserved there in the mud and become fossils. This fact led to my becoming involved in paleontology, the study of fossils, and before long I was serving as consultant to various geological institutions. One of the skills I had to acquire was a knowledge of anatomy, so that fragmented bones could be reassembled and identified. Some of the restored bones I produced in this way became the object of research by specialists, and various museums sought my aid in these matters.

Consequently when I learned by chance of the existence of hundreds of fragmented human bones taken from archaeological digs that had yielded artifacts on which I could see delicate inscriptions written in the Iberian alphabets of about 1000 B.C., I naturally became very interested and inquired whether the bones might be made available to me for study. They would be the first human remains we had yet encountered that were directly linked with grave sites from which readable inscriptions in an ancient European language were also recovered. Through the good offices of Dr. William P. Grigsby of the Tennessee Archaeological Society, I eventually found myself sorting, washing, and restoring the skulls of the former owners of the inscribed artifacts.

The first Americans, by which I mean people born and bred in the New World, certainly descended from migrants who entered North America by the only land route that links the Americas to the Old World, the now nonexistent land bridge of the Bering Strait. Whether the first humans, pithecanthropoids of the species *Homo erectus,* ever reached the New World is unknown. Their fossils span areas in Africa and Eurasia that are or were tropical and subtropical (as during interglacial phases in Europe). Since it is doubtful whether a suitably warm climate could have occurred in the latitude of the Bering Strait, especially at times when the sea level was low enough to enable a land bridge to develop, it is possible that the reason why no pithecanthropoids have been found in the Americas is because none ever reached here. By the time man had evolved to the stage represented by the Neanderthals of Europe, and the Old World generally, periods of low sea level were still occurring, and it seems evident that the bridge to America was crossed by humans on one (or many) of those occasions. Fossil man at the Neanderthal stage is now known from Brazil, and George Carter's latest (1980) estimate suggests that a conservative date for the entry of man into America might be about 100,000 years ago. How long people like Neanderthals may have survived in the New World is not known, but their cousins in the Old World were contemporaries of modern types of man, at least until about 40,000 B.C.

As to what kinds of man came next to America, opinions of the various anthropologists who have commented in recent years seem all to be much the same: that it is likely that pygmies were early entrants, since they once formed an important part of the southern Mongolian population, still linger on in isolated parts of Malaysia and neighboring territories, and are known by carbon-dating to range back in time to at least 40,000 B.C. Before these latter facts were known, writers such as Harold Gladwin, E. A. Hooton and Carleton Coon suggested that there are traces of former pygmy populations in America, mainly in the shape of isolated communities of undersized people on the offshore islands.

Others, such as the zoologist W. D. Funkhouser, and the physicist W. S. Webb, of the University of Kentucky, drew attention to the extraordinary diversity of skull form in the prehistoric burials of Kentucky, and proposed that several distinct races are represented. Bennett H. Young (1910) had encountered a living tradition among Kentucky folk that pygmies had once lived in some of the valleys of tributaries of the Mississippi in that state. But when he tried to track the stories to their source he concluded that they must have been based on a misinterpretation of the cist burials. The latter are small stone-slab burial containers, some three feet in length, into which the disarticulated bones of the dead were placed. The examples he saw did not disclose pygmy skeletons.

My interest in this problem was aroused in 1980. I was engaged on reconstructing the thousands of fragments of crania from sites in east Tennessee, sent to me by Dr. William P. Grigsby and his colleagues. Among the best of the materials they sent me from 600 burials were several fragmented but almost complete crania, with jaws, in which the brain capacity was that of a seven-year-old child (950 cubic cm), yet the teeth showed from their complete development and severe wear that the skulls were from middle-aged individuals. Later I received from Dr. Grigsby some complete skulls among which was one unbroken pygmy skull, with the jaws still attached to the facial bones.

As is often the case in Europe, prehistoric burial grounds from which these and other skeletons were recovered by members of the Tennessee Archaeological Society showed from their associated artifacts that a broad time span is implied, and that whereas some of the burials had occurred during the Woodland period (ranging back to about 1000 B.C.), others had taken place later. From the similar states of preservation of the bones of both the pygmy types and those of the other races present in the burials, it appeared that the pygmies were contemporary with the other races. I obtained permission to sacrifice some of the long bones of the limbs for radiocarbon dating. The result of a carbon-14 determination, with C-13 correction, made by Geochron Laboratories, Cambridge, on carbon dioxide recovered from the bone collagen yielded an age of 2,160 years plus or minus 135 years: that is, they dated from about the third century B.C.

The majority of the other skeletons conformed to the most common type of Amerindian anatomy, in which the head is of the rounded (brachycephalic) type, and the jaws project slightly (mesognathous), the lips therefore being full, as in many Western tribes today. This a typical Mongolian condition, and there could be little doubt that the population was derived from ancient forebears who had entered the Americas from Asia. Some of the skulls, however, were of a Europoid type, and reference by Dr. Grigsby to his very large collections (some 32,000) of stone and bone and pottery artifacts from the sites had already disclosed to him that inscriptions in old European scripts were engraved on some of the objects.

It looked, therefore, as if a mixed population of several races had lived in the east Tennessee area, and in all probability they would have interbred. No pygmies are known to have survived to modern times in North America, at least not in the United States or Canada, but it does seem likely that pygmies may have been among the native peoples encountered by the first European explorers to come to eastern North America.

Before I received the skeletal material I had already become interested in the problem of whether or not pygmies might have inhabited North America. The ancient European word for pygmy or dwarf is a root based on the form *nan-*. Thus in ancient Greek it is *nanos,* in Basque it is *nanu* or *nano* (according to dialect), in Irish Gaelic it is *nan,* and modern French has *nain,* Spanish *enano.* This strange unanimity among the various languages of Europe, not all of them closely related, seemed to suggest that there might once

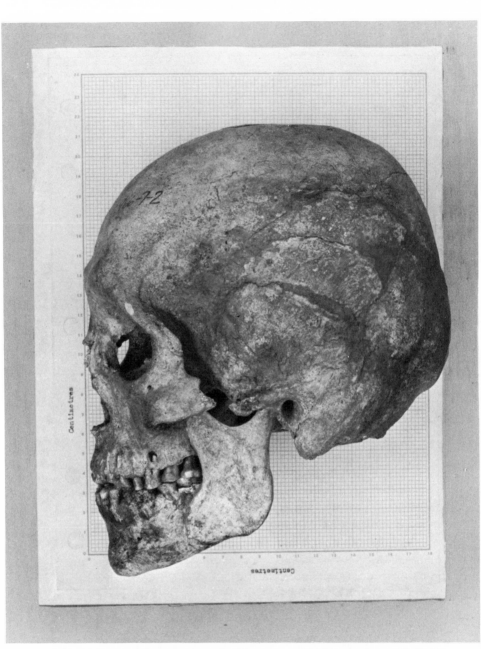

Figure 3-1. Two primary sources of evidence are available as to the racial affinities of the peoples who inhabited eastern North America at the epoch when the megalithic sites were in occupation. The first and major source of evidence comprises skeletons and skulls excavated from burials where the bones are found in association with artifacts that bear readable inscriptions. This skull, which closely resembles European types, is from Holliston Mills, east Tennessee. It exemplifies a racial type that occupied the region in early Woodland times and that is associated, at the neighboring site at Snapp's Bridge, with inscribed artifacts bearing Celtic and Basque words and phrases appropriate to the first millennium B.C. Similar remains from a mound near Boston have been amino-acid dated to ca. 5000 B.C., these apparently representing the earliest European Atlantic crossings. *Photo Walter Eitel.*

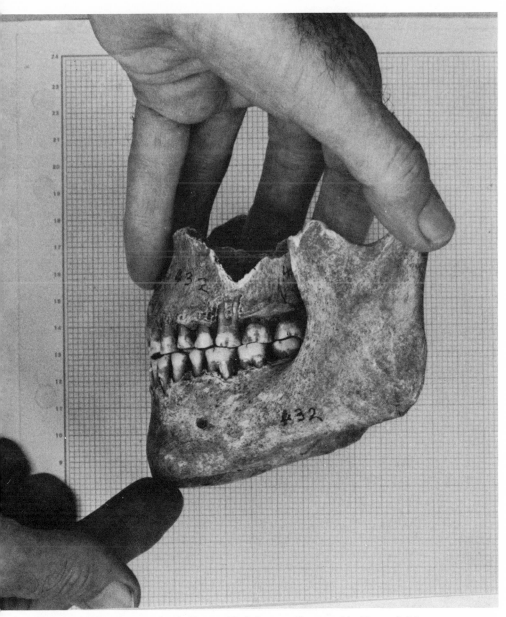

Figure 3-2. The most markedly Europoid of the type illustrated in Figure 3-1 have perfectly straight, vertical jaw profiles (orthognathous) and a stout vertical ascending ramus (hinge) to the lower jaw. This example is from Holliston Mills, Tennessee, and was excavated by the Tennessee Archaeological Society. *Photo Walter Eitel.*

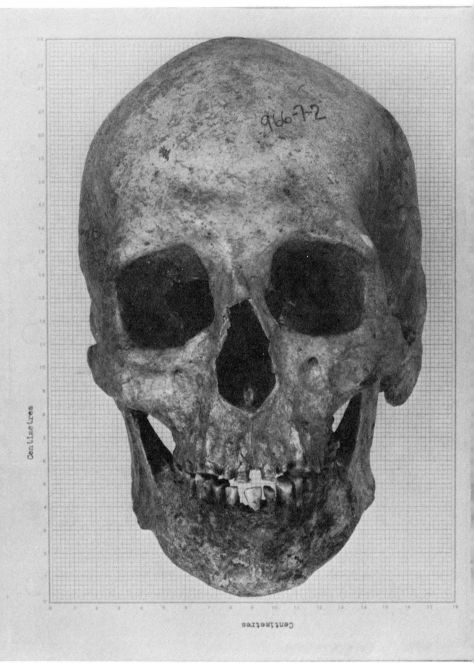

Figure 3-3. Views of the skull shown in Figure 3-4. The cranium is of medium length (mesocephalic). *Photo Walter Eitel.*

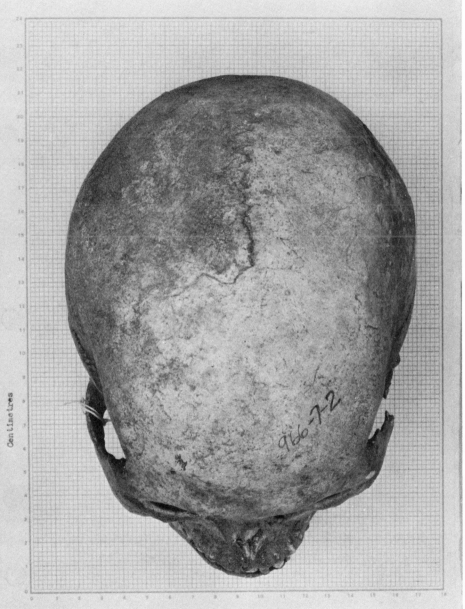

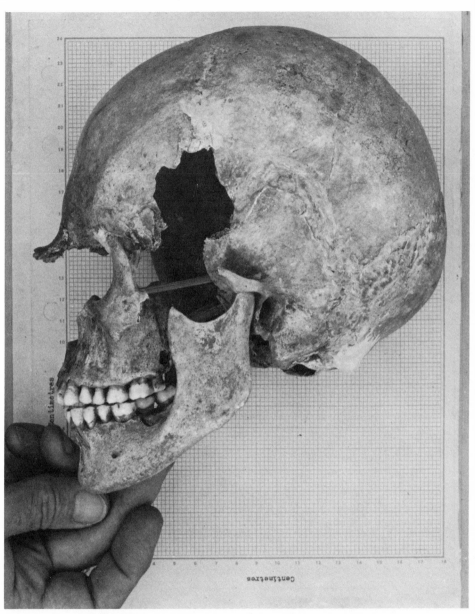

Figure 3-4. Skulls with moderately protrusive teeth, extending beyond the chin (mesognathous) and a rounded (mesocephalic) cranium match types of colonists who entered Spain and Portugal at the close of the Neolithic period. They may also have entered North America by way of the Bering Strait, using water-borne transportation. People with skulls like this (from Holliston Mills, Tennessee) may well have constituted the Algonquian population at the time when Woden-lithi and his fellows visited Canada. *Photo Walter Eitel.*

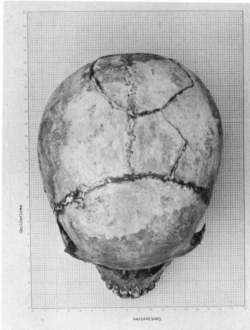

Figure 3-5. Long-headed (dolichocephalic) and round-headed (brachycephalic) types of Amerindian: both were present in east Tennessee, the former distributed in Canada and northward, the latter in the southeastern states. Many of these closely resemble the maritime Neolithic people of Mugem, Portugal, who frequented coasts and rivers, used the bone harpoon, and had domesticated the dog. *Photo Walter Eitel.*

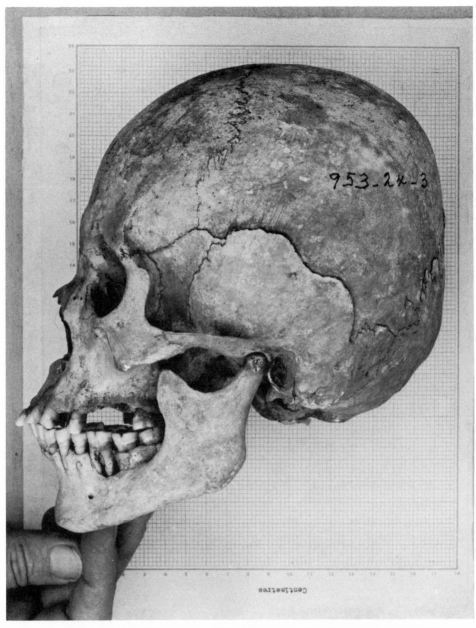

Figure 3-6. Also inhabiting parts of North America in the Bronze Age were pygmy types, some having a brain capacity equal to that of a seven-year-old child (950 cc), though their teeth showed that the cranium still had this small size when the individual was middle-aged. These pygmy types had round (brachycephalic) heads, with very conspicuous large projecting jaws (prognathous). These characteristics link them with the pygmies of Malaya and the Philippines, who probably originated in southern Mongolia. These types, though still living in east Tennessee as late as the first millennium B.C., range back in time to at least 40,000 years B.P. (carbon-dating establishes this).

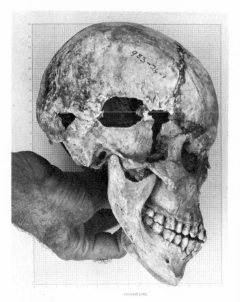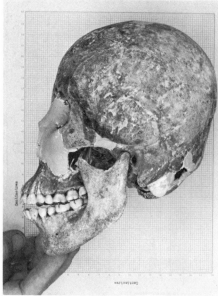

Figure 3-7. Two more examples of the pygmy type, both from Holliston Mills, east Tennessee, and both derived from the stock with prognathous jaws and a small rounded cranium. *Photo Walter Eitel.*

have been a race of pygmies known to ancient Europeans. The lack of pygmy bones in European archaeological sites seemed to imply that the inferred pygmies, if they existed at all, may not have been European pygmies. Yet it seemed inconceivable that ancient Europeans could have known about the pygmies of central Africa, or those of the remote highlands of Malaysia and the Philippines.

What intrigued me still more, and prompted me to draw attention to the matter in two papers I wrote on the language of the Takhelne tribe of British Columbia, was that these American Indians also had a tradition of pygmies (or dwarves), whom they called the *Et-nane*. Later I learned from a colleague that the Shoshone vocabulary also includes a similar word, whose root is *nana-* and is defined by the compiler of the *Shoshone Dictionary* as "elf-like people."

Now, when I began to analyze the anatomical characteristics of the pygmy skulls from Tennessee, I soon discovered that they matched those of the pygmies of the Philippines, who are also brachycephalic. Further, I learned from accounts of explorers in Malaysia who had penetrated to areas where no racial intermixture had occurred that the pure or true-bred pygmy there has very prognathous jaws, as is the case with the American skulls. These Malaysian and Philippine pygmies are regarded by archaeologists as remnants of a formerly extensive Mongoloid pygmy race that once occupied much of southern east Asia. Carter believes that their characters are still to be recognized in dilute trace form in the occasional frizzy hair, dark skin, and squat stature observed among southern Chinese. Significantly, perhaps, the best-known native name of the Oriental pygmies is the *Aëta*. Perhaps this root is the origin of the prefix *Et-* used by the Takhelne. Whether that be so or not, I think it is clear that the pygmies of Tennessee were of Oriental—that is to say, east Asian—origin; and since pygmies are not maritime people, they can have reached the Americas only by the land route.

They must once have been more widely dispersed than our present finds imply. However, since they reached as far east as east Tennessee, and their bones have been found in association with Europoids and inscribed artifacts of Europoid type, such as loom weights and pottery stamps, lettered in ancient Celtic and Basque, I conclude that there were in fact meetings of the two races, and that therefore the European visitors could well have taken back to Europe some account of these mysterious undersized people. An inscription that Professors Heizer and Martin Baumhoff had recorded from eastern California (Figure 3-11), when deciphered as Celtic ogam, seemed also to suggest that early explorers had encountered some pygmy race that they considered dangerous.

In addition to skeletal remains, a number of sculptures, evidently of ancient origin, have been discovered at varying depths in the soil, some of them depicting people of obvious Europoid origin, yet all the evidence indicates that these sculptures were created in America, at an era long before the colonists arrived in modern times. Some representative illustrations (Figures 3-8, 3-9, 3-10) may serve to show their nature and their similarity to ancient European sculpture that has been attributed to the Gauls. Most striking is the head of a man, carved in the Celtic style, with the curving nostrils and staring eyes that one encounters in Irish art and wearing as a chaplet a twig of bog oak leaves and acorns. It seems difficult to regard this as representing anything other than a Celtic priest, or druid. It was found in Searsmont, Maine, a part of a larger work of which the torso still remains on the site, the head being now in the museum at Sturbridge, Massachusetts, to whose director I am indebted for the information that the head exists.

It is my opinion that these heads and others like them are truly ancient American artifacts, and that the hands that carved them are also responsible for the engraved inscriptions in ogam and other ancient European alphabets, found on artifacts at burial sites and also cut in rock.

Figure 3-8. A second source of evidence are sculptures found by chance, usually in the course of industrial excavation or the excavation of house sites, in the region where megalithic chambers and dolmens occur; these supplement skulls and skeletons excavated by archaeologists together with associated artifacts, some of which carry inscriptions of the type that occur in Europe at Bronze Age or other pre-Roman sites. This head was discovered at Searsmont, Maine, executed in bedrock. It is now in the Sturbridge Museum, Massachusetts. It obviously depicts a Celt, as the artistic style (curving nostrils, staring eyes, chaplet of bog oak with acorn) all attest. *Photo Malcolm Pearson.*

Figure 3-9. This massive stone head, now on exhibit in the Peabody Museum, Salem, Massachusetts, was discovered at a depth of 10 feet in 1811, when foundations were being dug for a house at Essex, Massachusetts. It is twice life-size, and the style invites comparison with that of known Celtic sculpture, notably the sunken eye-sockets (as in a Breton style) and the straight narrow lips. Compare with Figure 3-10. *Photo James Whittall.*

Figure 3-10. Sculpted stone head, attributed to the Celts, found at Vannes, Brittany. The style recalls that of the preceding example, from Essex, Massachusetts.

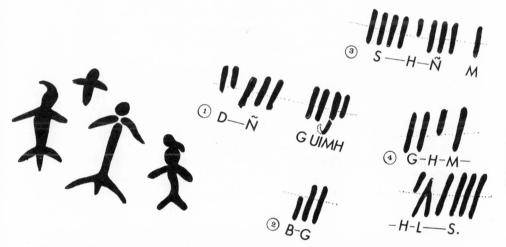

Figure 3-11. Decipherment of ogam script, Old Irish language, from east California, Inyo County, Site INY-430 of Heizer and Baumhoff.

A travelers' warning:

"*The men [here] are savages, small and ill nourished, but hostile.*"

Translation as follows:

D-N (Old Irish *doini*) men
GUIMH (Old Irish *goim*) of savage nature
B-G (Old Irish *beag, becc*) small
S-H-Ñ (Early Irish *seng*) ill-nourished
GH-MHL-S (Gaelic *gamhlas*) of hostile character
M (Gaelic *ma*) but

4
KING WODEN-LITHI
SPEAKS

Using Table 1, the comparisons of the Tifinag alphabet with the short inscriptions found in Sweden and Denmark, and supplementing these by the much more extensive material now recognized in America, it is not difficult to reconstitute King Woden-lithi's own alphabet. It is given in Table 2.

It is now possible for anyone who cares to do so to visit the site at Peterborough, Ontario, with this book in hand, and perhaps a copy of Geir T. Zoega's *Dictionary of Old Icelandic* (Oxford University Press, 1910) as an independent check, and to see and read the inscriptions the king had cut, and thus for the first time ever hear the words of a Bronze Age language that stands in the direct line of descent of English and the other Nordic tongues. Although nearly 4,000 years stand between us and King Woden-lithi, we can still recognize much of his language as a kind of ancient English. It is an eerie feeling to realize that we are reading, and hence hearing, the voice of the ancient explorers of Canada whose thoughts now come to us across the space of forty centuries, yet still with familiar words and expressions that remain a part of the Teutonic heritage.

This is not the place to instruct readers in the grammar of Old Norse, let alone the still more obscure grammar of Bronze Age Norse, but it is quite within the realm of practical life for visitors, including teachers and their students, to examine for themselves at least the more conspicuous and best preserved of Woden-lithi's recorded comments. The diagrams in this book will make this task relatively easy. And for those who wish to make independent

Sign	Sound	Initial letter of	Sign	Sound	Initial letter of
∧, ⊓	d	dyrr (doorway)	⊖	b	bukla (shield, buckler)
○	hr	hringr (ring) ◇⊡) also written	‖ ∘∘	l	liki (equal, like)
⟩	m	mán (moon)	⊙	s	sol (sun)
⦵, ⊟	w	waettir (weights)	∘ ∘ ∘ ∘	h	Hestemerki (Pegasus) (the square of 4 stars that form the constellation)
⦂∘	k	kuml (cairn, heap)	∘ ∘ ∘	gh	ghomr (roof beams)
⊔⊔	th	thili (planks, partitition)	⅔⅔	y	Yorsa (Cassiopeia) (the W-shaped group of stars that form the constellation)
⎮	n	naddr (nail)	⊏	p	par (a pair)
⩊	f	far (ferry boat)	⋋	r	rifa (to split)
⬇	t	tagg (barbed arrow)	⌐	gn	gneipa (bent) (alternatively the sign may represent a bat-ax, from root *gnr*, battle).
⊢⊣	tz	zaun (railing, fence)			

Table 2.

Inferred origin of the Tifinag alphabet. While it is impossible to relate the Tifinag signs to the natural appearance of objects whose initial letters are those of the Tifinag alphabet, if the Berber language be regarded as the original tongue of the inventors of the alphabet, a very natural derivation emerges if the Tifinag letters are related to the Nordic names of objects that they resemble. Hence it is inferred that the script originated with Nordic speakers and then subsquently became the adoptive script of Berbers. Scribes often write the letters upside down, sideways, or in mirror image.

checks, or to translate parts of the text that are not included in this book, there can be no better guides than Zoega's *Dictionary,* a grammar of Old Norse such as E. V. Gordon's (Oxford University Press, 1927), and a camera to record the inscriptions for more detailed study at home. For many of the words an Anglo-Saxon dictionary will also aid recognition.

The easiest parts of Woden-lithi's text are, of course, those where the letters are engraved on the largest scale, and that therefore have suffered least from the erosion of time and the elements. One of the clearest sections is located about 30 feet to the west of the central sun figure. The individual letters are from 20 to 40 cm high, and they form a horizontal band about 5 feet (1.5 m) long. The inscription lies directly beneath the figure of the god of war, Tziw, and it is in fact a dedication to this god. The god can be recognized from illustrations 9-1 and 9-2, and by the fact that he stands beside the Fenrir wolf, which has just bitten off his left hand. This Norse myth is discussed in chapters 9 and 13. For the present we will restrict ourselves to the line of dedication, shown in illustration 9-2. With the exception of the ornamental capital TZ that begins the name of the god, all the letters are easily recognizable from the table of Woden-lithi's alphabet in, *Table 2.* Remember that vowels are nearly always omitted in all Bronze Age inscriptions except when they occur at the beginning of a word, or where possible confusion of meaning might result. The line of text of the dedication reads:

W-K   H-L-GN   TZ-W   W-D-N-L-T-YA

The last two letters are written in ogam and form a rebus of a ship, on the right, all the others are in Bronze Age Tifinag. The meaning of the text is "Image dedicated sacred to TZiw by Woden-lithi." The individual words are as follows.

W-K, matching Old English (Anglo-Saxon) *wig,* a heathen idol, in this case a bas-relief ground into limestone, depicting the god. Probably we have to supply the same vowel, *i,* to make the letters *w* and *k* pronounceable, *g* and *k* are related consonants, both formed in the throat; the only difference is that *g* requires the vocal cords to reverberate (as can be felt by placing the fingers on the throat when uttering the sound of *g*), while in pronouncing *k* the vocal cords remain inactive, so no vibration is felt on the throat. Jakob Grimm, the great German philologist, first showed how pairs of consonants, such as *g* and *k d* and *t, b* and *p,* change (mutate) from voiced to unvoiced if they occur in certain positions in words. Woden-lithi apparently spoke with an incipient "German" accent, and preferred to use a *k* at the end of words where we in English are usually content to retain the ancient *g* sound.

The next word, rendered by Wodenlithi's scribe as H-L-GN, means *hallowed* or, as we would prefer to say in modern English, *dedicated.* It is a root that is common to all the Teutonic languages. Germans, for example, retain it to this very day as *heilig,* meaning *holy,* which in turn is another modern English word derived from H-L-GN. In the Scandinavian languages the word survives unchanged, as *helgen,* meaning *holy* or *to make holy,* and the Anglo-Saxon form of the word is represented by such old terms as *halig* (holy), *halgan* (a saint), *halgung* (a consecration or dedication), with *hallow, hallowing, Halloween* (All-Saints' Eve) as surviving English derivatives. Halloween is the night before the first day of the ancient Nordic winter (November 1), when ghosts were reputed to roam at large. These spirits could be bought off, by bribes, from any evil intentions during the following year, hence our modern surviving custom of giving token gifts to children dressed as demons and ghosts. The children of Woden-lithi's Ontario settlers no doubt carried on the same custom.

The next word is the name of the god himself, here rendered as *TZ-W.* This implies a pronunciation similar to the ancient German name of the god of war, Tziwaz. Our Anglo-Saxon forebears called him *Tiw,* and in the Middle Ages the surviving form of the name, in the word *Tuesday,* became what we still say today, for the god of war is still commemorated by having the second day after the sun god's day named for him.

The last word is the name of King Woden-lithi himself, and it is written beside a pictograph of a man wearing a robe and crown, to show the reader that the word is the personal name of a king. Elsewhere in the various texts on the site we find the word king spelled out in Tifinag, and it then has the form *konungn,* matching Anglo-Saxon *cyning,* Old Norse *konungr* and other similar forms in all the Teutonic languages. *Lithi,* here rendered as *litya,* means "servant," thus the king's name is "Servant of Woden." Woden was the king of the Aesir or sky gods.

The dedication to Tziw illustrates the way in which we can use dictionaries of Anglo-Saxon or Old Norse, as well as modern English dictionaries that give the old roots (such as the *OED* or the *American Heritage*), not only as a guide to understanding what Woden-lithi is saying, but also as a means of guessing approximately what his language—our ancestors' language—actually must have sounded like.

It is not needful here to continue treating in detail the rest of the numerous texts that lie about the site at Peterborough and at other places such as the sites along the Milk River, Alberta, or in Coral Gardens, Wyoming. Readers can devise their own philological checks, if these interest them, or ignore the subject if they are more interested in other aspects. This chapter has shown how to approach the ancient inscriptions.

Now that we have seen that the alphabet really does give us the means of reading the various texts that King Woden-lithi had engraved at the Peterborough site, when he selected it for the sacred center of his colony, I should like to make some comments on the origin of this alphabet.

It is, as I have said, essentially the same alphabet as that used by the Tuareg Berbers. A possible reason for this surprising circumstance is suggested in Chapter 17. However, neither I nor any of the other scholars who have worked on Tifinag inscriptions in North Africa could ever understand the relationship between the Tifinag alphabet and the Berber language. It has now become clear that there is no relationship. Tifinag is *not* a Berber invention—instead it is *Nordic*—and that changes the whole problem.

The decipherment of any ancient and unknown inscription requires first that the alphabet in which it is written must be solved. Various methods can be used to achieve this first essential. In the case of Woden-lithi's inscription I found the solution relatively easy, for I had previously traveled widely in the Scandinavian countries, where shorter but similar inscriptions occur on Bronze Age monuments, and I had also carried out research on the ancient scripts of

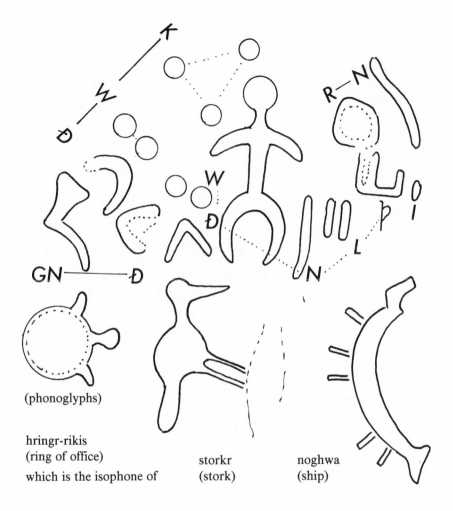

(phonoglyphs)

hringr-rikis
(ring of office)

which is the isophone of

storkr
(stork)

noghwa
(ship)

Ringerike Stor Konogna

Figure 4-1. The opening phrases of Woden-lithi's inscription are rendered partly in Tifinag letters, and partly in an older hieroglyphic style, called phonoglyphs, in which pictographs give an approximation to the sound of the words intended. In the above passage the reading intended is

W-D-N-L-I-TH-I Ringerika stor konungr K-W-D R-N GN-D

(*Woden-lithi, Ringerika stor konungr kweid runa gneid,* "Woden-lithi, of Ringerike the great king, instructed that runes be engraved"). Rubbing stones found at the site showed that the inscription had been abraded into the limestone by rubbing, as the inscription here implies, as the verb *gneid* means literally to rub.

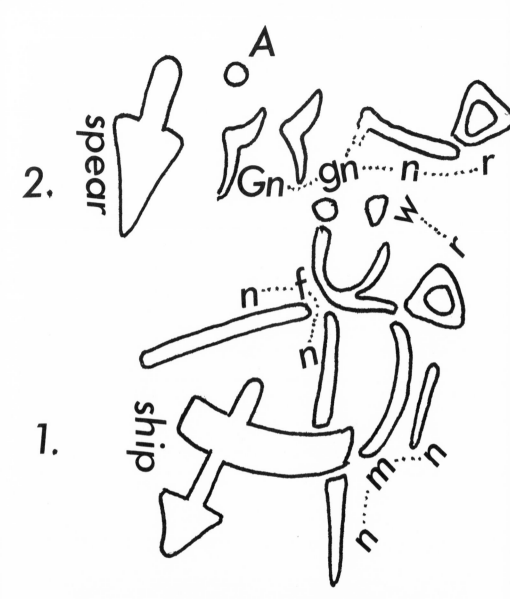

Figure 4-2. After identifying himself and his kingdom in Norway, the king next tells us the name of his ship. The symbols for *spear* and *ship* are determinatives, telling us the category of objects to which each of the alphabetic names applies. Thus GN-GN-N-R (Old Norse *gungnir*) is a name given to a spear, in this case the famous magic spear of the sky god Woden; and this name was then given to a ship, shown hieroglyphically by a pictograph of a ship. The inscription is to be read from bottom to top, each line reading from left to right, as follows:

1. *Skip niman* (A ship he took)
2. *A-Gungnir war nefn* (In-honor-of-Gungnir was its name).

Therefore, the Norwegian vessel *Gungnir* is the earliest ship known by name to have reached the Americas, she sailed the St. Lawrence River, and was commanded by Woden-lithi, High-King of Ringerike, the ancient capital of Norway.

The section of Woden-lithi's text shown here can be located about 18 feet southwest of the main sun-god figure at the Peterborough site.

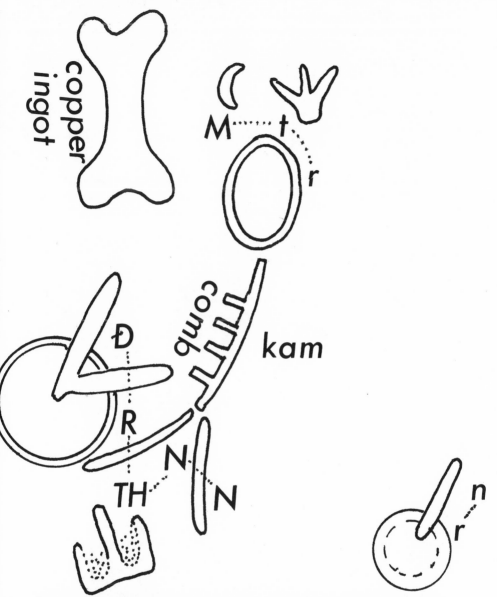

Figure 4-3. The king now tells us the purpose of his visit to Canada. Two hiero-glyphic symbols appear in this section. The copper ingot symbol is universal in Bronze Age inscriptions, and originated in Mesopotamia, where ingots were cast in the shape indicated by the sign. Numerous examples of the sign are also known from American inscriptions and Amerindian token money (see *Saga America*). The other hieroglyph, a comb, is peculiarly Norse. A comb in Norse was called *kam*, and *kam* also happens to be the past tense of the verb to come, *komu*. Thus an ideogram of a comb yields the sound of the verb *came*. The text reads:

> For ingot-copper of excellent quality (Old Norse *maetr*)
> came (Old Norse *kam*) the king (Old Norse *drottinnin*)
> by way of trial (Old Norse *reyna*).

This section of the text lies to the left of the preceding section, which is about 18 feet southwest of the main sun-god figure.

In modern terms the king would have said that his voyage was a test run for market research.

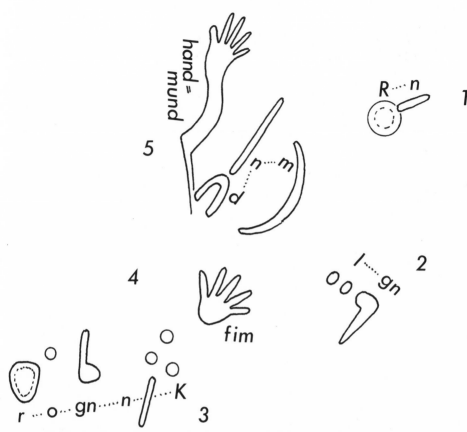

Figure 4-4. The king now tells us how long he stayed in America. The next part of the text (illustration that follows this one) specifies the actual months. Two hieroglyphs occur in this section. One, the five fingers, is merely the numeral 5. The other, an arm and hand, represents the word *mund* (Old Norse, a hand), which in turn is an isophone (punning word sounding the same as another word) for *manad* (Old Norse, month). In this section the word for *king* (Old Norse *konungr*) that was given hieroglyphically at the very start of the inscription (Figure 4-1) is here spelled out in Tifinag letters. The text here reads in a clockwise swing from 1 to 5:

(R-N Old Norse *reyna*) As a trial the king (K-N-GN-O-R) lay at anchor (L-GN, Old Norse *lagna*) for five (Old Norse *fim*) months (M-N-D).

This section of the inscription occurs just beneath the preceding section.

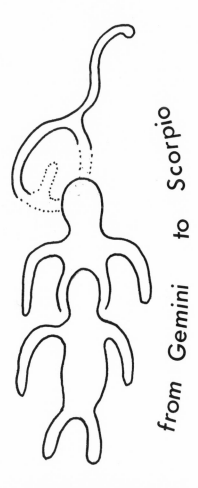

Figure 4-5. The text until now has been descending vertically down the rock face. After taking the clockwise swing in the previous section, it now ascends the rock face immediately to the left of the preceding sections.

Here the king specifies the actual months he was present in Canada, by naming the signs of the zodiac occupied by the sun. He came when the sun was in Gemini (in 1700 B.C. this would be April–May, for the vernal equinox lay between Taurus and Aries; see Chapter 5). He departed for his home in Norway when the sun was in Scorpio, meaning August–September, for the intervening sign of Libra was not inserted into the zodiac until about 300 B.C. The sign for Scorpio is partly eroded here, but reference to the complete zodiac, as given in Woden-lithi's astronomical text, shows what form he gave it (see Chapter 5).

The significance of this section is to specify the months mentioned in the previous section. It is to be read as meaning:

From April–May until August–September.

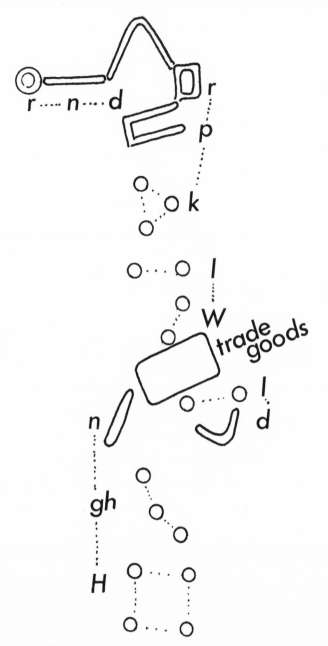

Figure 4-6. As the text now ascends the rock face the king tells us how he spent those five months "dealing profitably with the foreigners, exchanging his trade goods for copper ingots." The "foreigners" were the resident Algonquians, whose friendly welcome Woden-lithi had elsewhere recorded (see Chapter 1).

Two hieroglyphs appear in this section, and both are still used by the Algonquians: a square sign stands for trade goods, and a meandering sign means "expedition." Woden-lithi, however, contrives to spell out the word, while still forming a rebus winding trail from its components. The text reads:

> *Hagna* (Profitably) *del* (he dealt) [trade
> goods] *wal* (with the foreign people) *ko-
> par* (for copper) *erandi* (the object of the
> expedition).

The modern English word *errand* is cognate with *erandi*.

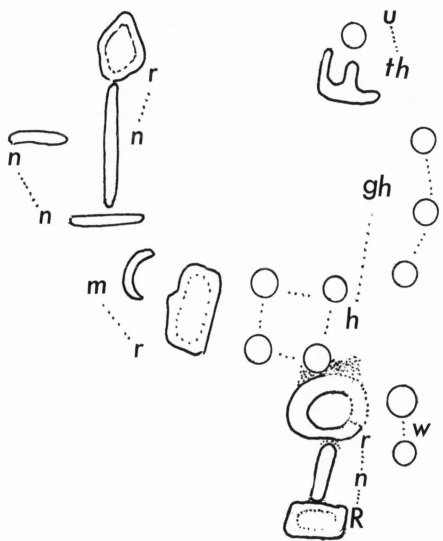

Figure 4-7. The narrative portion of the king's inscription concludes in this section, which lies above the preceding part and, like it, reads in ascending sequence. All the letters here are Tifinag. The text reads:

> R-N-R (Old Norse *runar*, Runes) W (Old Norse *va*, in [this] secluded nook) H-GH (Old Norse *hokk*, he hacked) U-TH (Old Norse *uti*, out) N-R (Old Norse *nara*, while he lingered) N-N (Old Norse *nain*, near) R-M (Old Norse, *rum*, this place).

The rest of Woden-lithi's inscriptions deal, for the most part, with calendar regulation and astronomy, religious festivals, Nordic mythology, and standards of measures.

North Africa, including the Tifinag of the Tuaregs. The Tuaregs had preserved their unique system of writing since time immemorial, and its origin was unknown, though all epigraphers, including me, supposed it to have been their own invention.

Four thousand years ago the ancestors of the present-day peoples who speak Teutonic languages were all grouped together in Scandinavia, in parts of Germany, and along the Baltic coasts. They had not yet differentiated into Germans, English, Norse, so we can refer to them only as Nordic. Their descendants today not only live in northern Europe but have spread across the world, and most people in North America now speak a tongue directly descended from the ancient Nordic of the Bronze Age.

Although short inscriptions in the ancient Nordic alphabet have recently been recognized in Scandinavia, that discovery stemmed from the more significant one of ancient Nordic engraved on North American rock. Thus North America has now become custodian of the oldest and most precious of the ancient records of the Nordic peoples, and to Canada is assigned the responsibility of preserving them intact, and the thanks of millions of people must go to the geologists, surveyors, and archaeologists who uncovered the main site and placed it under the protection of the local government. For myself I have also to thank Otto Devitt, who first drew my attention to the site and has since photographed it carefully to aid my decipherment.

Our ancestors of the Nordic Bronze Age inherited some of the signs of their alphabet from their Neolithic predecessors, who also spoke a Nordic tongue and used a number of signs. Thus the following signs were already known in northern Europe before the Bronze Age, and we now know that they give the sounds shown in Table 2.

As is quite obvious, these are hieroglyphs in which the signs depict recognizable objects, and the sound they stand for is that of the first letter in the name of the object. Thus, the crescent that is *m* is obviously the first letter of *mán,* the older form of our modern English *moon.* Similarly the circular sign *r,* or *hr,* is the first letter of the word *hringr,* meaning our modern word *ring.* So also the circle with a dot in the center, *s,* is the first letter of *sol* and of *sunu,* the two ancient Nordic names of the sun. The *b* symbol is clearly the old Nordic *buklr,* the circular shield with a leather arm-strap, which is still called a *buckler* in modern English. These four signs, with the indicated sound values, were needed by the Neolithic wizards to indicate certain words that mean magic (*bur-* in Proto-Nordic), sailing ship (also *bur-*, though a different root), and the combinations of these two words with signs for the sun and moon, both of which were viewed as celestial gods that sailed their sun ship and moon ship by magic across the heavens. Simple statements of this kind can now be read, by sound as well as by pictograph, in the Neolithic engravings on rock in Scandinavia and also in North America, as far west as California.

The German philologist Jakob Grimm traveled among the village communities of Germany and the Baltic lands 150 years ago, and discovered old words such as those I have mentioned. He used his findings to develop a forecast of modern theories on how language evolves through time. He also recorded the old names of the constellations. This is fortunate for us, for when we look at the deciphered Nordic alphabet of the Bronze Age we can now recognize more of the origins of the alphabet. For just as the letters *s* and *m* reflect the form of the sun and the crescent moon, so also we now perceive that the dots that make up other letters, in a kind of Braille system, are really the constellations.

Thus, as I have explained in *America B.C.,* just as the ancient Celts gazed at their fingers and invented a writing system called *ogam* based on the varying combinations of five strokes above, below, and across a central writing axis, so also the ancient Nordic people gazed instead at the sky and saw their letters writ large upon the face of heaven. No doubt they said their script was divine, sent from the sky by the sky god Woden (Odin), lord of magic and of runes, the secret writing of the magicians. As this word *runes* has already been applied to later types of writing developed by the Norsemen after the Iron Age, we cannot use it without some qualification for our Bronze Age alphabet, to which it undoubtedly was originally applied. So we have to compromise and call the oldest writing of the Nordic peoples Bronze Age runes.

There remain a number of other letters that seem to be formed from more commonplace objects of everyday life in ancient times. Table 2, with my suggestions as to these origins, explains itself.

In my previous popular books on North American inscriptions I was faced with the difficulty of trying to explain to an English-speaking public the meaning and language of texts engraved in tongues so remotely different from English that it made the tasks both of writing the books and of reading them (as many correspondents have told me) decidedly difficult.

Now, thanks to King Woden-lithi, these problems all vanish. He spoke and wrote a language that resounds down the centuries with the age-old familiar tones of all the Nordic tongues. We speakers of English, as well as our cousins in Europe who speak related languages, can all recognize many of the words that Woden-lithi and his Ontario colonists spoke and wrote here seventeen centuries before Julius Caesar first encountered the Nordic tribesmen of the Rhineland.

Although Woden-lithi's site at Peterborough is the first recognizable Nordic Bronze Age site to be discovered in America, it now appears that there were other visitors from the Nordic world of that era. For some years a puzzling inscription has been known from little Crow Island, near Deer Isle, Maine, but it could not be deciphered, nor was the script recognized. It is shown in Figure 4-8 and in Figure 4-9 a provisional reading is given, which suggests that some voyager from Scandinavia, seemingly named Hako or Haakon, visited Maine at a time when the Bronze Age runes were still in use. This inscription greatly resembles the script called *bead ogam,* but the resultant text, if it be read as bead ogam, is gibberish, whereas if we treat it as Tifinag script, a Nordic text, although rather obscure, emerges. The lack of associated pictographs or hieroglyphs increases the difficulty of reading the signs.

Figure 4-8. This inscription at Crow Island in Penobscot Bay, near Deer Isle, Maine, has been known, for several years, but until the recognition of Nordic Tifinag script in 1981, its meaning could not be determined. A proposed decipherment is given in the following illustration. *Photo Malcolm Pearson, 1977.*

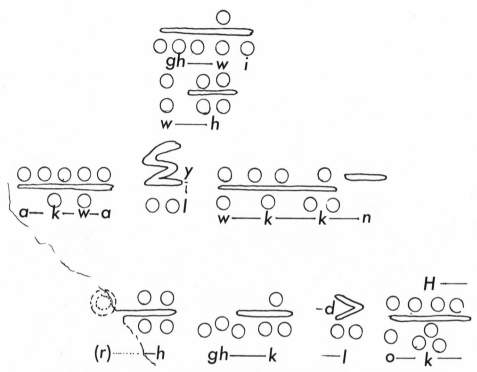

Figure 4-9. Weathering and the lack of associated isophones or other determinants makes the decipherment of the preceding inscription difficult. In the above proposed reading, the text is read from right to left on each line. Allowing for vagaries of spelling, it apparently is intended to read: *Ey vik hvi nokkvi leya a vika. Hako lod kugga her*, "A sheltered island, where ships may lie in a harbor. Haakon brought his cog here."

5
KING WODEN-LITHI'S
OBSERVATORY

To the discerning eye the solar observatory that King Woden-lithi established at his trading center near Peterborough is one of the wonders of American archaeology. So surprising do his knowledge of the constellations and his understanding of the motions of the sun through the signs of the zodiac appear that at first it seems impossible that the site could be ancient. It is more like what one might expect to have been constructed during the early Middle Ages. However, consideration of what has been discovered about the growth of astronomy shows that it is not at all impossible for Woden-lithi to have known what he did know and yet have lived in an epoch 3,500 years before our own.

Until about a century ago, all that we knew about ancient astronomy was what the Greeks and Romans had written. It was supposed that the Greeks had named the constellations, and that therefore man's knowledge of the stars as mapped in the constellations could not be older than about 2,700 or 2,800 years; for some of the constellations, and their roles in setting the time of year for plowing, sowing and reaping, are mentioned by name in the works of Hesiod, the first Greek writer to refer to them, who lived about 800 B.C.

Then an unexpected discovery was made. Archaeologists in the Middle East began to uncover tablets of stone in which clear reference was made to constellations, some of them recognizably the same as those we know today, yet the age of the records extended many centuries earlier, into a time antecedent to the Greek civilization.

An English astronomer, Richard Proctor, devised an ingenious method of finding out when the constellations first received their names. He plotted on a chart all the constellations known to the ancients. He then examined the area in the sky, over the Southern Hemisphere, in which no constellations had been recorded until modern astronomers named them, because the Southern Hemisphere had not been explored by the ancient astronomers. He found that this southern blank area has its center, not at the southern celestial pole, as one might expect, but in quite a different place: a point in the southern sky some 25 degrees to one side of the South Pole. When he realized that this center must once have been the pole, at the time when the constellations were named, he then attacked the related question, the known motions of the poles as the earth's axis has slowly wobbled like that of a spinning top. He found that the ancient position of the poles he had discovered, for the time when the constellations were named, corresponded to a direction of the earth's axis that was correct 4,000 years ago. Thus, the constellations must have been named some 2,000 years before the time of Christ. It was then discovered that the description of some features of the sun's motion in the sky, given by a Greek astronomer named Eudoxus, could not possibly have been true at the time when Eudoxus wrote, but would have been correct had he been quoting from sources dating back to 2000 B.C. The position of the sun at the time of the vernal equinox (in March) was recorded by these early writers as lying in the zodiacal constellation of the Bull. But in classical times, when Eudoxus wrote, the vernal equinox occurred when the sun is in the constellation of the Ram, some 30 degrees away.

What this means for us is that when the Nordic farmers first learned the arts of sowing seed by the calendar, and could thereby be sure of seeing the seed sprout instead of rotting in the ground, as would happen if it were not sown at the correct time, this phase of social history in the northern lands matched the rise of astronomy, around 2000 B.C. Evidently the astronomical skills passed along the same trade routes as did the trade goods themselves: from the Danube and the Rhine there spread outward and northward into Germany, and then Scandinavia, a knowledge of the constellations and the motion of the sun through them. Observatories would be established to watch for the equinoctial rising of the sun and for other significant astronomical events that could be used to keep the calendar correct and functional.

Hence it was one of the concerns of Woden-lithi in America to ensure that his colonists were provided with a practical means of observing the sky and the heavenly bodies, so that they could have always a reliable farmers' calendar. Certain religious festivals were also regulated by the calendar, such as the spring (New Year) festival in March, and the midwinter or Yule festival held in December.

To establish his observatory, Woden-lithi had first to determine the position of the north-south meridian of his site. He probably used the following method. First, he selected a central observing point, and engraved two concentric circles into the rock (thus forming the head and central "eye" of what later became the main sun-god image). An assistant then held a vertical rod, centered in the marker circles, on a clear day as the sun approached its noon altitude. The shadow cast by the vertical rod would grow shorter as the sun rose higher, and then would begin to lengthen again as the sun passed the highest elevation at noon, and commenced to decline. The direction of the shadow at its shortest length was marked on the rock. Checks on subsequent days would establish this shadow line more precisely. The marked line, except for minor errors due to variations in the velocity of the earth's motion (for which no correction could be made in those early days), would be the meridian, running north and south.

Woden-lithi could now lay out the cardinal directions, north, south, east, and west, by making a right-angle intersection with the meridian line, to give the east-west axis (see Figure 5-1). Instead of cutting lines for these cardinal axes, however, he made sighting points at their extremities, by cutting sunburst figures, as shown.

The sighting sunburst for due east he then identified by an inscription lettered in ogam consaine, shown on the right side of Figure 5-1. In his Old Nordic language it reads M-D O-S-D-N (Old Norse *mot osten,* facing east). The illustration gives a plan view to the scale shown, so the visitor can readily identify these features at the site.

At this stage in his work Woden-lithi had now provided his colonists with the fundamental tool for regulating their calendar,

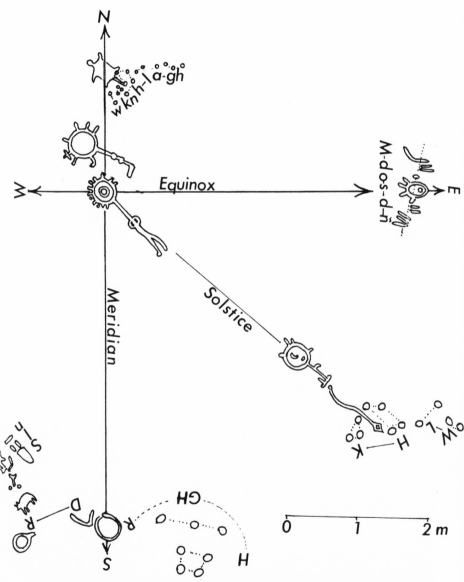

Figure 5-1. Plan view, to scale shown below, of the calendar observatory established by King Woden-lithi on the meridian of 78° W, near latitude 44° 35 N, near Peterborough, Ontario. For explanation of the Old Nordic text inscribed on the axes, see Chapter 5.

for, every year at the vernal equinox in March, when the ancient year began for all civilized peoples, an observer standing on the site would see the sun rise at a point on the horizon lying on the line of sight from the "eye" of the central sun-god figure to the eastern sunburst figure. On that occasion each year the Nordic peoples held a festival, named for the goddess of the dawn, Eostre. The name survives in our modern language as *Easter,* now of course linked with a Christian festival to which the old pagan name has been attached.

Ancient peoples also celebrated another festival on the shortest day of the year, called by the Nordic nations *Yule;* this pagan festival is nowadays linked with the Christian festival of Christmas, still called Yule (spelled *Jul*) in the Scandinavian countries. Woden-lithi therefore wished to provide his colonists with a means of determining the day on which the Yule feast should be held, for to the ancient peoples it was a great day of celebration, marking the end of the sun's winter decline and the promise of a new and warmer season ahead.

Woden-lithi's inscriptions tell us that he remained in Canada only for five months and that he returned to his home in Scandinavia in October. Hence he could not observe the direction in which the sunrise would be observed on the actual day of midwinter, for he was no longer in Canada. So apparently he estimated the direction, drawing on his experience in Scandinavia. In southern Norway the precise direction of sunrise on Midwinter Day varies quite considerably, for at the latitudes spanned by the interval between the southern end of the Skagerrak (at about 56° N) and the head of Oslo Fjord (at 60° N), the astronomical equation that determines the sunrise direction gives solutions that range over a span of some seven degrees between the extreme values. Consequently, since Woden-lithi probably did not have any clear conception of latitude, and would have to judge the situation in terms of his notions of the variations seen in Norway itself and neighboring Sweden, he would probably conclude that the Peterborough site seemed to be comparable with southernmost Scandinavia. For example, he would have noticed that the midday sun stood higher in the sky at midsummer at Peterborough (when he was present to observe) than it did in his homeland, and he would also know that the noonday sun stands higher in the southern Sweden than it does near Oslo on any given day. From such knowledge he perhaps estimated the likely sunrise direction for Midwinter Day, and cut his estimated axis into the rock at the site. This he marked by another sun-god figure (which I have labeled *Solstice* on Figure 5-1). Woden-lithi himself had a label carved into the rock beside this figure. As can be seen from the illustration, it spells W-L H-K. *Hoki* was the ancient Norse name of the midwinter festival: the word still survives today in the Scotch word *Hogmanay,* the traditional name of the Scottish midwinter holiday, now applied to the New Year holiday. The letters W-L evidently represent the *hvil* of Old Norse, meaning a time of rest, a holiday from work. The importance of this *Hoki* holiday can be judged from the large scale in which the letters have been engraved at the site. It was, no doubt, the time of the major national festival for all Nordic peoples, and Woden-lithi undoubtedly intended that the old traditions be kept alive in his trading colony in the New World.

As we examine the site today, where these ancient instructions for regulating the calendar year and its festivals still survive, it is clear that whereas the critical date for starting the year and determining the correct time of planting seed, the equinox, is accurately set out, the same is not true of the *Hoki* axis. It overestimates the southern declination of the sun by several degrees. Woden-lithi's colonists would find that the midwinter sunrise did not, in fact, ever range quite so far south as the king had predicted, and that the sunrise point would begin to return toward the eastern horizon before ever reaching the southeastern azimuth to which Woden-lithi's *Hoki* axis now points. Nonetheless the general tenor of the matter would be clear enough, and since most years the midwinter sunrise tends to occur in banks of low-lying cloud, the error was probably known to only a few of the more meticulous observers.

As I have already pointed out in *America B.C.,* those of us who have made the somewhat hazardous journey to observe the midwinter sunrise at sites in the Green Mountains that are oriented for this purpose, have discovered the whole area under the deepest snowdrifts. The same circumstance, no doubt, is true of Woden-lithi's site: the whole inscription area, with all the astronomical axes, would usually lie buried under deep snow, hence invisible and useless for making astronomical determinations of the festival dates.

I think the explanation of these conflicts of data is to be sought in our developing knowledge of climatic change. In Woden-lithi's time the whole earth had a much milder climate than it did one thousand years later. The site at Peterborough may well have been prairie rather than dense needle-forest, as it is at present. Open views of the distant horizon could be had, the actual sunrise could be observed, and because of the milder climate, the snow, if present at all, could be cleared away from the site.

I also think that as the climate deteriorated with the progress of time, the people here at the end of the Bronze Age, around 800 B.C., began to find the snow an increasing impediment to their calendar regulation. They were forced to construct a new type of observatory, one that could retain its major astronomical axes in a visible and usable state despite the snow accumulations. These new observatories were, I believe, the stone chambers described in Chapter 2, where the observers could be housed comfortably below ground, with a large living space that could be heated by fire, and with the axis of the entire chamber directed toward the midwinter-sunrise azimuth on the distant horizon, so that the calendar observation could be made simply by sighting from the inner end of the chamber, through the entrance doorway, which was built so as to face the midwinter sunrise point. Once this practice had been adopted to overcome the ferocity of the winters, reaching its extremes of discomfort as the Iron Age began, the advantages of astronomically oriented chambers would be realized, and soon all observatories, whether based on summer, equinoctial, or winter sunrise directions, would eventually be constructed as comfortable chambers. The old open-air sites, like that of Woden-lithi, would be abandoned forever, become buried under drifting soil and leaves and then turf (as happened at Peterborough), or would be eroded away by the elements till nothing readable remained, and thus disappear altogether.

To return to Woden-lithi's site, it is of interest to note that he adopted the ancient *Semitic* method of naming the south direction. The Semitic peoples regarded east as the main map direction. Facing east they would name the cardinal points on either side, so that north became "left-hand" and south became "right-hand." On Woden-lithi's site we find that he has engraved in very large Tifinag letters the word H-GH-R at the southern extremity of the platform, where he has cut yet another sunburst figure. The word intended is Old Norse *hogr*, meaning "right-hand." The word is still used today in Sweden where, if you are given street directions in Stockholm or Lund, you are sure to be told to take such and such a turn *till högra*, "to the right." The Danes say *højre*, but we who speak English seem to have lost the word, and replaced it by another root. The Old Norse words for south (*sudhra*) and north (*nord*) are nowhere to be found on Woden-lithi's site, so far as I can ascertain; perhaps they had not yet come into use.

Now, since we find Woden-lithi using the Semitic (Mesopotamian) methods of naming directions by reference to the right and left when facing east, and since east is the only direction that he actually calls by its special name, east (*osten* in his dialect), it is not surprising that we should find Woden-lithi in possession of so much information on the Babylonian maps of the heavens, as designated in the form of the named constellations.

Constellations Known to Woden-lithi

The first hint we encounter on the observatory site that the stars were already grouped into constellations in Woden-lithi's day is given by the northern end of his meridian (see Figure 5-1). Here we find an inscription in Tifinag that reads W-K-N H-L A-GH, and it is evidently to be read as Old Norse *Vagn hjul aka*, "The wagon-wheel drives." The constellation near the present north celestial pole that we in America call the Big Dipper today, and which Europeans often call the Plow or Wain, was known to our Nordic ancestors as the Wagon. It was supposed to be an ox wagon (that is, the ancient chariot, before horses had been tamed) and was said to be driven by the god Odin, the Woden of our colonists. In Woden-lithi's day the north celestial pole was marked by the star Thuban, in the constellation Draco; nowadays it lies some 25 degrees away from the pole. The Wagon was conceived as wheeling around and around the Pole Star. The wheeling motion, of course, is caused by the rotation of the earth, but in Woden-lithi's day it was conceived as a rotation of the sky itself. We have other hints, as mentioned in

Chapter 4, about star groups known by name to the peoples of the north in Woden-lithi's time: the four stars that form the square of Pegasus (called *Hestemerki,* "horse-sign," by the ancient Norse) seem to be the basis of the four dots that make the Tifinag letter *h;* and the *w*-shaped group of stars that form Cassiopeia, called *Yorsla* by the ancient Scandinavians, seem to be the origin of the *w*-shaped letter that gives the sound of Y.

To the southwest of Woden-lithi's observatory lies an area of limestone where the constellations of the Nordic zodiac have been engraved. These are shown in Figures 5-2 and 5-3. We note that some of the Babylonian constellations bear replacement names in the Woden-lithi's version. The Ram (Aries) is obviously a bear, and some broken letters beside the image of the animal seem to spell in Tifinag the word B-R-N, a root that appears in all Nordic tongues in one form or another, as *bjorn* in Scandinavian, and *bruin* in English. The next sign, the Bull (Taurus) of classical astronomy, is drawn as a moose; it is labeled in Tifinag L-GN, Old Norse *elgen,* the elk. The Lion (Leo), though labeled L-N (Old Norse *leon*), seems to have been carved by an artist who had in mind a lynx. The Crab (Cancer) looks like a lobster, and it is drawn as if it lies at the feet of the Twins (Gemini), here identified as M-T TH-W-L-N-GN (Old Norse *matig-tvillingr,* "the mighty twins").

The significance to Woden-lithi's people of the zodiac was that it provided a means of describing the annual path of the sun through the heavens. The sun spends about one month in each of twelve constellations, which together form the so-called zodiac (a word meaning "girdle of animals"). The vernal equinox, the start of the ancient Nordic year, occurs at the time when the sun is located in the zodiacal sign for that equinox. Two thousand years before Christ, when, as we have seen, the constellations received their names, the sun occupied the Bull (the elk in Woden-lithi's zodiac). Around 1700 B.C. the slow wobble of the earth's axis (called the procession of the equinoxes) caused the vernal equinox position to move out of the Bull into the neighboring sign, Aries (in Woden-lithi's terminology, the bear). In Woden-lithi's zodiac map he shows the situation in just that way. The word W-GN (Old Norse *vaegn,* a balance) signifies the "balance of night and day," and is set opposite

Figure 5-2. First section of the ancient Nordic zodiac, from Aries (shown as a bear), through Taurus (shown as an elk), to Gemini and Cancer. The equinox is marked between Taurus and Aries, indicating a date of ca. 1700 B.C. The portion shown lies 15 feet south-southwest of the main sun figure. Peterborough, Ontario. For explanation of the Nordic words, see text of this chapter.

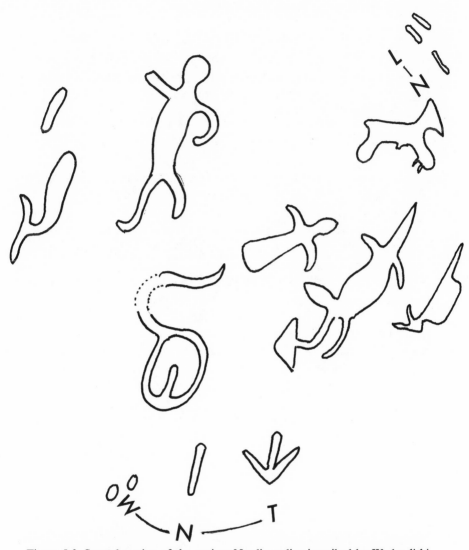

Figure 5-3. Second section of the ancient Nordic zodiac inscribed by Woden-lithi at his Peterborough observatory. Only the Lion (L - N. Old Norse *leon*) is identified in Tifinag script. From upper right Leo (seemingly a lynx), and beneath to its left, the virgin, Virgo. Then follow the zodiacal signs for winter, identified as W-N-T (Old Norse *vintr*), which are Scorpio to the lower left of Virgo, Sagittarius, the archer, and Capricornus, the sea-goat, both to the lower right; and upper left Aquarius, the water-carrier, and Pisces, the fishes. The sign for Libra (scales) does not appear in any zodiac before ca. 300 B.C., when it was formed from the claws of the scorpion. The archer, in all the oldest zodiacs, appears as a centaur carrying a bow, as seems to be the intention in this zodiac. The signs are not arranged strictly in accordance with their sequence, probably because the only part of the zodiac of concern in calendar regulation at that era was the equinoctial point between Aries and Taurus.

the space between Taurus and Aries. In addition, as can be seen on the right-hand side of Figure 5-2, the sun is shown entering the W-R-M zone of the zodiac at that point. The word intended is simply our word *warm,* Old Norse *varm,* meaning summer. On the part of the zodiac corresponding to the sun's positions during the cold months the engraver has written the letters W-N-T, our word *winter,* Old Norse *vintr.* All the indications are, then, that Woden-lithi used a chart of the sky that was appropriate in 1700 B.C. Since his writing system and the style of his inscriptions match so well the inscriptions that Scandinavian archaeologists declare to belong to the early Bronze Age, we may assume that Woden-lithi did in fact live around that time. Hence, until evidence is found to the contrary, I believe we have to date his visit to America as having occurred around 1700 B.C.

There are other indications that this is a reasonable estimate. Some archaeologists who have investigated the site have suggested a possible age of 3,500 years, based on the similarity of the art style to that of Europe 3,500 years ago. At a neighboring site in Ontario where a thousand or so copper artifacts were excavated, radiocarbon dating indicated occupation a thousand years before the time I propose for Woden-lithi: that is, around 3000 B.C. And some of the radiocarbon dates from the Lake Superior copper mines indicate that the mines were worked between about 3000 and 2000 B.C. All these data suggest that the copper-mining industry was already an old established activity in Canada long before Woden-lithi came to trade for copper.

Stone Circles

Yet another form of calendar site has come under investigation in recent years: the circles of standing stones that occur in large numbers in Europe and also span the entire continent of North America from New England to California. A variant form in America, especially in western Canada and the adjacent United States territories, such as Wyoming, is the stone circles with radial lines of boulders forming spokes to the outer rim, hence the name Medicine Wheel. In some cases it is believed that the spokes are oriented toward points on the horizon that were formerly the positions of the rising or setting of conspicuous stars, which could be used to mark the seasons. These star-rise and star-set positions can be calculated for particular epochs in the past, making use of the known equations that describe the motions of the earth's axis.

One of the best-known sites is Mystery Hill at North Salem, New Hampshire, mentioned in Chapter 2. Apart from the numerous stone chambers on the site there is also a stone circle. The circle, like many others now becoming known, has been encroached upon by the native forest, but radial avenues have been cleared to permit visitors to sight the major standing stones from the central observation platform. As the diagram (Figure 5-4) shows, there are five principal standing stones, four of which are still standing erect. The fifth has fallen over. One stone marks the meridian and lies due north of the central observation point. The other four mark the sunrise and sunset points on the horizon for the midsummer and midwinter solstices. On account of persistent distant cloudbanks on the horizon the actual moment of contact of the rim of the sun is often invisible for, at the moment when the ball of the sun is about to reach the marker stone, it vanishes into mist. However, about once every eight or ten years a totally clear sunset or sunrise can be expected, and on such an occasion the event is truly impressive. On the diagram (Figure 5-4), in which Osborn Stone assisted by reading the exact azimuths from his transit telescope, the observed angles are those shown; their deviation from the theoretical calculated values is only of the order of minutes of arc. It is obvious that the site is an ancient astronomical observatory for the regulation of the calendar, whatever else it may have been. To judge by the modern solstice ceremonies of Amerindian tribes, one may assume that much religious import was also attributed to the celestial phenomena by the ancient peoples who would assemble at the site to participate. At Mystery Hill the major significance seems to have been the summer and winter solstices, and regulation of the calendar by the vernal and autumnal equinoxes does not seem to have been an important part of the purpose of the ritual.

There are also many sites, as yet little known or wholly unrecorded, where a dozen or so natural boulders form ring-shaped structures. They vary from small circles, such as one that occurs at

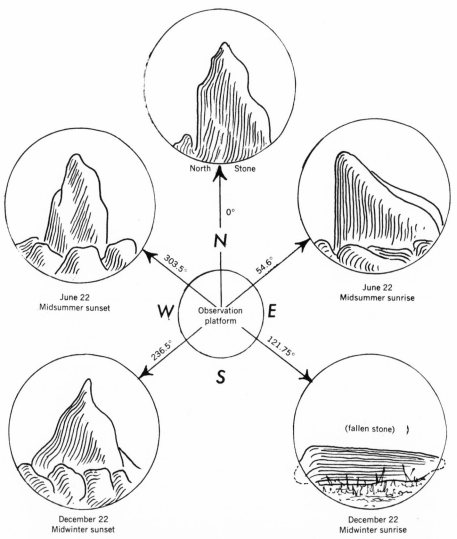

Figure 5-4. Azimuth directions of the major standing stones at the Mystery Hill stone circle in New Hampshire. The observed directions coincide, to within an accuracy of some minutes of arc, with the sunrise and sunset bearings at the summer and winter solstices, as indicated.

Gungywamp near Groton, Connecticut, to rings of more massive boulders, up to 15 meters in diameter, that would have involved considerable labor in assembling the giant stones in this manner. One photographed by Jerry McMillan in the Santa Cruz Mountains, California, is shown in the photograph in Figure 5-6. An approximate plan of the thirteen stones forming it is seen in Figure 5-5. These rings seem to have been places of assembly for religious purposes; whether they also served as astronomical observatories (as seems very probable) remains yet to be proven. Jerry McMillan and Christopher Caswell discovered and photographed old engraved markings on two of the stones; these have not yet been deciphered but they seem to record angles of sight.

Some of the smaller rings of stones that are found in the Sierras and in Montana do not seem to me to be calendar sites. They remind me of the old *shielings* of the Scottish Highlands. A shieling was a place on the open mountainside where the young women of a clan would gather in spring, when the herds were in flow, to make cheeses and other milk products. They slept in the open, in shelters provided by such rings of stones, which remain today as witness to a way of life that has vanished from Scotland. It was still practiced a century ago, and when I was a student in Scotland in the 1930s I met aged women who had participated in the shieling and who had a stock of folklore to relate on the subject (the Devil himself being one of the personages liable to frequent the shielings, on the watch for any careless maiden who might not have said the necessary protective charms).

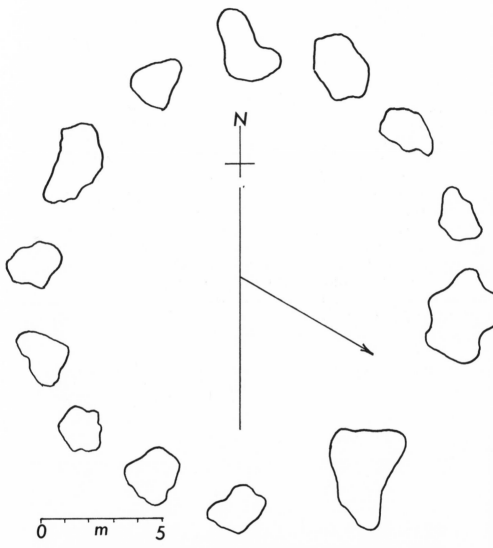

Figure 5-5. Plan of the stone circle at Big Basin, Santa Cruz Mountains, California, as drawn by Jerry McMillan in 1981. The circle, some 15 meters in diameter, comprises 13 stones, with the meridional axis as shown. On the southeast bearing (lower right) two larger stones mark the direction of the winter solstice sunrise on December 21.

Figure 5-6. View approximately toward the west, stone circle at Big Basin, Santa Cruz Mountains, California. The site is overgrown by forest. *Photo Jerry McMillan.*

Figure 5-7. Some stone circles can be associated with specific roles other than astronomical, as at Trelleborg, Sweden, where the central dolmen suggests that the entire structure, ring included, is for a funerary monument. *Photo Joseph D. Germano.*

6
BRONZE AGE RELIGION

As no Nordic inscriptions older than the Iron Age have hitherto been deciphered, King Woden-lithi's commentary on his gods is not only the first information we have had on the matter, but it is unique. The era in which he lived, calculated from the position of the vernal equinox on his zodiac as about 1700 B.C., is regarded as early Bronze Age in Britain, but in Scandinavia, where metals were imported, the Neolithic continued longer, and Woden-lithi would be regarded as living in the transitional time between the end of the Stone Age and the beginning of the Bronze Age, a period, often called Chalcolithic, when copper was employed.

Archaeologists and mythologists have concluded from a study of the carvings left by northern European peoples that sun worship was the religion practiced at this transitional phase and that it continued well into the Bronze Age. Their inferences are totally confirmed by Woden-lithi's inscription.

It is obvious that sun worship was the vogue, as the sun figure is placed at the center of Woden-lithi's sacred site, is drawn on a larger scale than the other figures, save only that of the moon goddess, and the lettering beside each of these deities is much larger than the other parts of the text (Figure 6-1).

The great festivals of the Nordic year in Woden-lithi's day were, as I have pointed out, those of Yule and of Eostre. At these times, as the inscription tells us, there was feasting and drinking, and men dressed up as comic figures called *Yule-men*. Their costume suggested the diagonals that mark the solstice and equinox lines on an azimuth plate recording the greatest and least excursions of the sun northward in the course of a year. Some of the actors

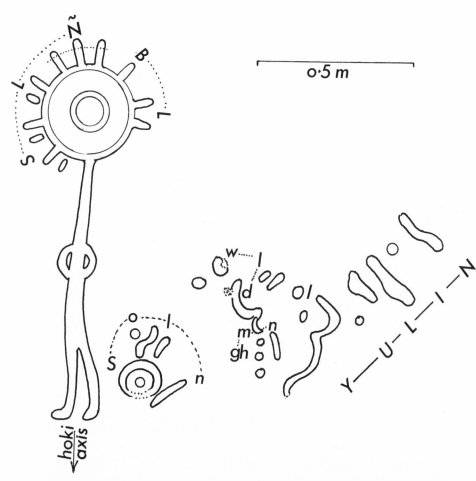

Figure 6-1. The main sun-god figure, at the central sighting point of King Woden-lithi's observatory. The elongated figure of the god lies along the *hoki* axis (direction of sunrise at Hogmanay), and the inscription may be read as S-O-L-N (Old Norse *solen*, the sun) and W-L-D GH-M-N L, Y-U-L-I-N (Old Norse *hvild gaman oll, Julinn*, holiday for rest and games for all, the Yule festival). Norse ogam on the disk of the sun spells S-L-N B-L, *Solen-bal*, "blazing sun."

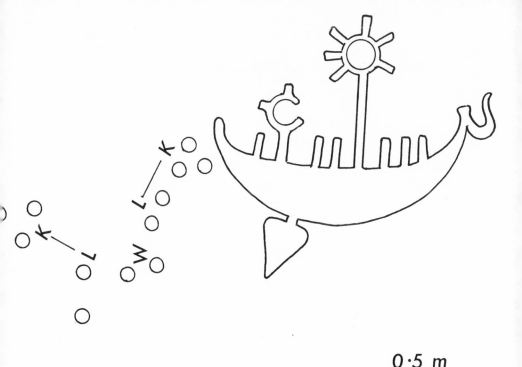

Figure 6-2. The solar ship, which carries the sun across the heavens each day and beneath the earth each night, is here depicted 12 feet southeast-by-east of the main sun-god figure. The inscription, a palindrome reading in either direction, is K-L W L-K, *Keolwe loki* (Old Norse *kjol ve logi*, "Ship of the Blazing Standard". The sun itself forms the standard. The Tifinag letters puzzled the archaeologists who originally uncovered the inscription; they recorded it as a "curved line of dots."

wore horns, others had outsize rabbit or hare ears. Some were dressed as other animals, and some performed acrobatics. Thus, the mad March Hare and the Easter Bunny of some Christian secular celebrations may be survivals from Woden-lithi's time, over 3,000 years ago.

If there was a lunar festival, whatever Woden-lithi may have said about that has not yet been recognized or deciphered.

Other gods are mentioned, but they seem to have been relatively minor nature spirits. These latter are divided into two groups, the more important *Aesir* (also sky gods, but having roles to play on earth and in the thinking of the people), the less important *Wanir* or earth gods, and the enemies of the gods, the giants and monsters of the underworld (including the bed of the ocean). These lesser divinities match their more important later derivatives, the gods of the late Bronze Age and subsequent periods.

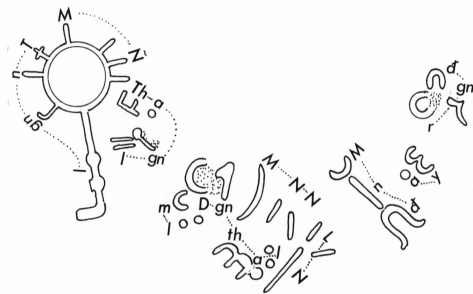

Figure 6-3. The moon-goddess figure lies to the right of the main sun-god figure at the Peterborough site. To the right of the moon goddess are the letters TH-A-GN-L (Old Norse *tungl*, moon). Below, center, M-L D-GN-TH-L (Old Norse *mal dagnatal*, measures the tally of days). To the right of that appears M-N-N L-N M-N-D A-Y R-GN-D (Old Norse *maninn luna, manadha ei reiknadha*, The moon, or luna, the months forever being counted). The disk of the moon goddess carries, on the right side, the Norse ogam letters M-N (*man*, moon), and on the left side Norse Tifinag letters T-N-GN-L (Old Norse *tungl*, moon).

Here is a list of the various divinities whose names have so far been deciphered on Wodenlithi's inscribed rock platform.

Major Divinities and Supernatural Monsters of Norse Bronze Age Religion

Name	Function	Other information
Sol	sun god	Governs the calendar and farming. A male god whose major festival is held on December 21 at the winter solstice. The festival, Yule, a time of general rejoicing
Mán or Luna	moon goddess	Governs the measurement of time.
Woden	a sky god	One of the *Aesir,* all sky gods. In charge of feasting, war, and death.
Loki	a sky god	An ill-natured but clever trickster, feared rather than worshipped. A son of Woden and father of monsters
Tiw	a sky god	In charge of war. He supports the heavens. Son of Woden
Thunor	a sky god	Strong and good-natured. He fights monsters and causes rain, and the thunder is the sound of his hammer, Molnir. Corresponds to the Norse Thor and Roman Jupiter
The Wanir	earth gods	*Frey,* male god of fertility, and his sister Freya, goddess of female fertility
Ymir	underworld god	Inhabits the sea, a giant, feared not worshipped
Fenri	underworld monster	A giant wolf that fights the gods of upper earth
Sleipnir	a magic steed	Property of Woden
Dwarves	underworld spirits	With magical powers and technical skills
Midgardsorm	underworld monster	Enemy of the gods, a giant serpent

The above list is not complete but probably includes all the major figures of King Woden-lithi's pantheon, the sky gods outranking those listed below them, and the sun, moon, and equinox gods standing above sky gods, the sun being lord of all.

The custom of having clowns, and in particular those buffoons that the inscriptions at the Peterborough site call Yule-men (see Figure 6-4), may have originated in Spain, for several sites are known in that country where images occur of humans dressed in this manner. The lowermost figure on the right depicts a woman dressed as a Yule clown, a feature not found at Woden-lithi's site; the Spanish Yule-lady shown here is from the Cueva de los Letteras. The upper left figure is lettered in Tifinag, and announces himself as a Y-L M-N, one of the Yule-men; it can be found about 5 feet northwest of the main sun-god figure. The other two Yule-men shown on the right side of the illustration are respectively from 14 feet and 16 feet northwest of the main sun-god figure. The two figures on the lower left lie about 50 feet southwest of the sun god. One is evidently a tumbler, the other a jackrabbit or, in terms of his European origins, a hare. In Scandinavia to this day the equivalent of Santa Claus is called the Yule-man (though nowadays he wears Icelandic costume, as does our own American Santa). The Scandinavian Yule-man also has a troop of Jule-nisser (Yule Dwarves) who accompany him. The hare seems to have vanished from the midwinter festival of modern times, and remains with us in the guise of the Easter Rabbit who now brings the Easter eggs, another survival of old Nordic pagan customs.

There are other links with ancient Spain, though not at Woden-lithi's site, which is predominantly Scandinavian. Figures 6-5, 6-6, and 6-7 show sculptures of animals that have been found in parts of New England where the stone chambers occur. The bison (Figure 6-5) is from Lawrence, in the valley of the Merrimack River in Massachusetts. It recalls the numerous Iberian sculptures, often crude as in this case, of bulls. The boar (Figure 6-7) and the recumbent beast, apparently a bull (Figure 6-6) were both discovered in central Vermont by John Williams and me while we were investigating the chambers at South Woodstock. They too recall the ancient Spanish sculptures.

The carvings in stone in northern Portugal also include numerous examples of animals, so much so that Professor Santos Junior, President of the Anthropological Society of Portugal (Sociedade de Antropologia e Etnologia de Portugal), has inferred that a special zoolatry (religious worship of animals) took place

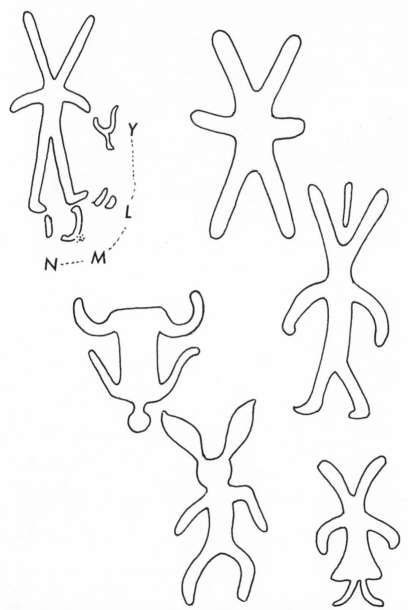

Figure 6-4. Yule-men from the Mid-Winter Festival as held at King Woden-lithi's site at Peterborough. On the lower right is a "Yule-woman" from the Cueva de los Letteras, Spain.

Figure 6-5. Bison sculpture discovered in the valley of the Merrimack River, near Lawrence, Massachusetts. The style, and the occurrence in a region where mega-lithic chambers and dolmens occur, suggests comparison with corresponding crude statues of bulls found in Spain and Portugal and especially in regions where Basque inscriptions, written in ancient syllabic script, occur. Professor Santos Junior has suggested that these statues imply a former religious veneration for certain animals (zoolatry). *Photo Malcolm B. Pearson*

Figure 6-6. Crude and time-worn image of a recumbent beast, apparently a bull, discovered near Woodstock, Vermont, by John Williams, in association with other evidence of megalithic remains. Like the preceding figure, this also suggests a link with the inferred ancient Basque animal worship. *Photo Joseph D. Germano.*

Figure 6-7. The wild boar of Iberia was one of the animals revered by the ancient Iberians in connection with their zoolatry. This eroded sculpture was discovered by John Williams and the author in the Woodstock area, near a large stone chamber axially oriented to the winter solstice. It appears to represent a boar or a sow. *Photo Peter Garfall.*

there. One of the examples he found was attached to a stone tablet carrying an inscription, which he sent to me. Like others from the region, where Basque place names occur, the inscription proved to be written in the ancient Basque tongue, using the ancient Basque syllabary (Figure 6-8). The inscription disclosed that it was a dedication to the Laminak, subterranean monsters that are still the object of superstitious dread among the Basque country people today.

It is relevant to state here that when Basque and other Spanish scholars sent these undeciphered inscriptions to me, nothing was known in Spain or Portugal as to the language of the writing. The solution (Figures 6-10 and 6-11) proved to be one that depended wholly on the fact that the Cree, the Ojibway, and some other Amerindian tribes have preserved this same syllabary today, and still use it in their letters, their newspapers, and other contexts. It is mistakenly attributed to the missionary James Evans, a Welshman who is supposed to have "invented" the script in 1841. What Evans really did, as I have pointed out in *Saga America,* was to preserve and adopt the writing system that he found already in use among his flock. For this he deserves great credit, but it is wrong to say he invented the syllabary. The system of writing goes back far beyond the earliest Roman inscriptions in Spain and Portugal. It continued in use among Basques until some time in the early Middle Ages. The last known example of its use is on a tablet now held in the San Telmo Museum (Figures 6-10 and 6-11). Using the Cree syllabary as a guide, I transliterated the signs into the phonetic equivalents in Latin script, and then recognized the language as Basque. Its translation appeared to be that shown in the illustrations, and I submitted my decipherment of the tablets to Dr. Imanol Agíre, the Basque etymologist and epigrapher. He confirmed the decipherment and provided a modern Basque rendering of the same text. (This, of course, is in marked contrast to the views of those archaeologists who state that the Basque inscriptions found in America are marks made by roots or by plowshares. For the views of linguistic scholars on the one hand, and archaeologists on the other, reference may be made to volume 9 of the Epigraphic Society's Occasional Publications, entitled *Archaeology and Epigraphy: Confrontation in America* [1981]). A possible means of Iberian influence on the Nordic settlements in Canada may have been the Algonquians. For, as an in-

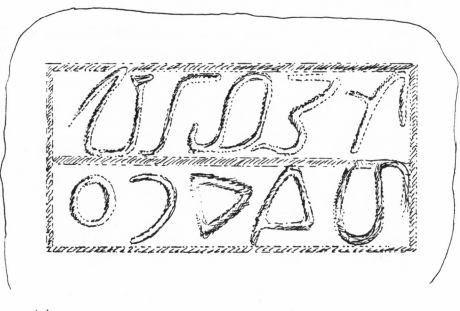

(1)   La ——— mi ——— no ——— ya ——— ri

(2)   o ——— to   e ——— gi ——— ni .

Translation
(1) To the Laminak (ogres)
(2) make prayer offerings.

Figure 6-8. This previously undeciphered stele was reported by Professor Santos Junior, president of the Sociedade de Antropologia e Etnologia. It was associated with numerous stone images of animals, found in the district of Berroes in northeast Portugal, adjacent to a dolmen-bearing zone where early Basque inscriptions were disclosed by my decipherments. This stele also is Basque, written in the Euskera syllabary. The Laminak (plural of Lamina) are usually stated by present-day Basques to be "mountain dwarfs," still feared in country districts of the Basque lands. But the great Basque scholar and lexicographer Resurrección María de Azukue cites the word as having the sense of *pythoness* or priestess where it is used in the Basque Bible, and other ancient sources speak of them as female monsters that inhabited the Basque lands prior to the coming of Christianity. Professor Santos Junior regards his finds as implying the worship of beasts in ancient Iberia (Santos Junior, 1977), especially at Tras-os-Montes. Perhaps the Laminak are in some way connected with this religion.

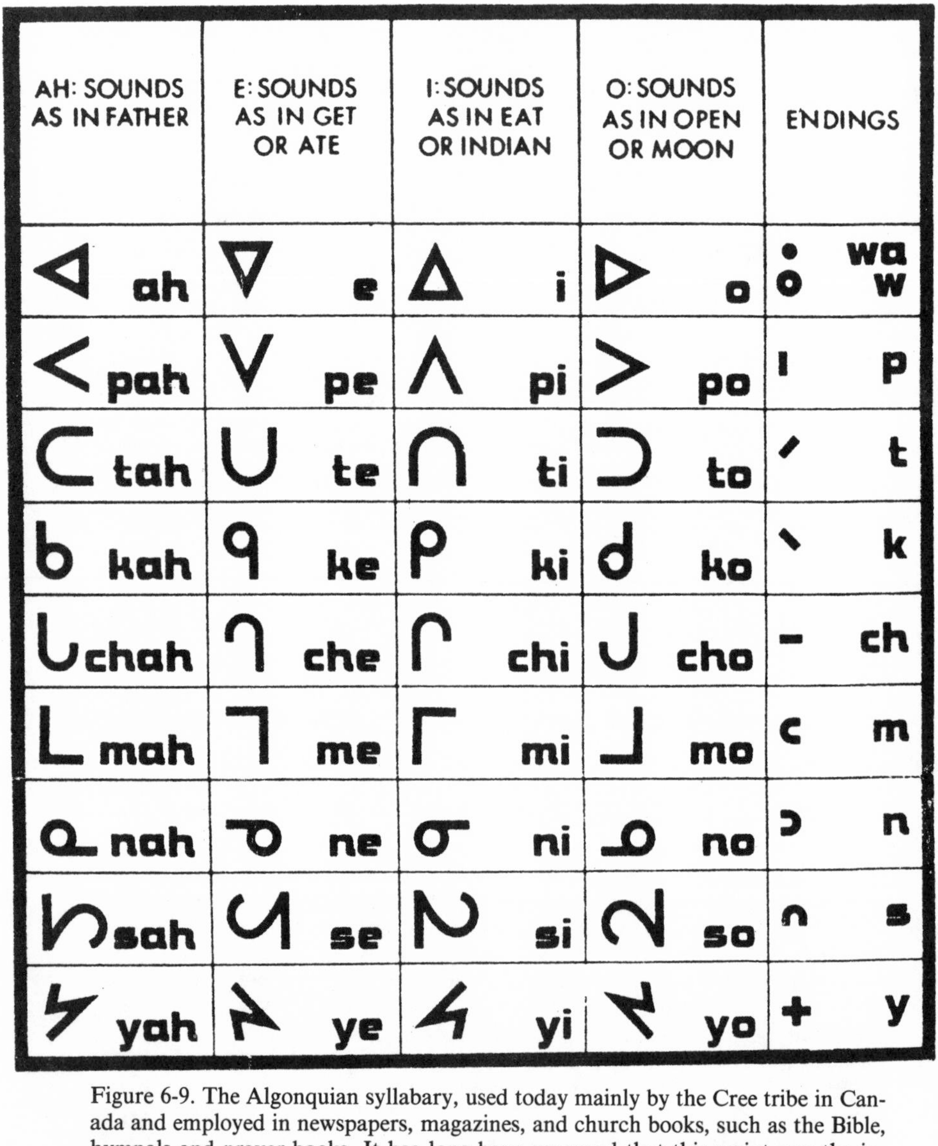

AH: SOUNDS AS IN FATHER	E: SOUNDS AS IN GET OR ATE	I: SOUNDS AS IN EAT OR INDIAN	O: SOUNDS AS IN OPEN OR MOON	ENDINGS	
◁ ah	▽ e	△ i	▷ o	• ● o	wa w
< pah	V pe	∧ pi	> po	I	P
C tah	U te	∩ ti	⊃ to	✓	t
b kah	9 ke	P ki	d ko	`	k
U chah	∩ che	Γ chi	U cho	–	ch
L mah	⌐ me	Γ mi	⌐ mo	c	m
Q nah	⌐ᴏ ne	ᴏ⁻ ni	⌐ᴏ no	Ɔ	n
∿ sah	⌐ se	2 si	∿ so	∩	s
⅄ yah	⅄ ye	⅄ yi	⅄ yo	+	y

Figure 6-9. The Algonquian syllabary, used today mainly by the Cree tribe in Canada and employed in newspapers, magazines, and church books, such as the Bible, hymnals and prayer books. It has long been supposed that this script was the invention of a missionary, James Evans, in 1841. In reality, as inscriptions from pre-Roman Spain and also on the Peterborough site in Canada show, the script is of very ancient origin and is due to Basques. The Basque inscriptions in Spain and Portugal were deciphered in 1979 by the author with the aid of the Algonquian syllabary. The decipherments have been confirmed by the eminent Basque scholar Imanol Agiŕe.

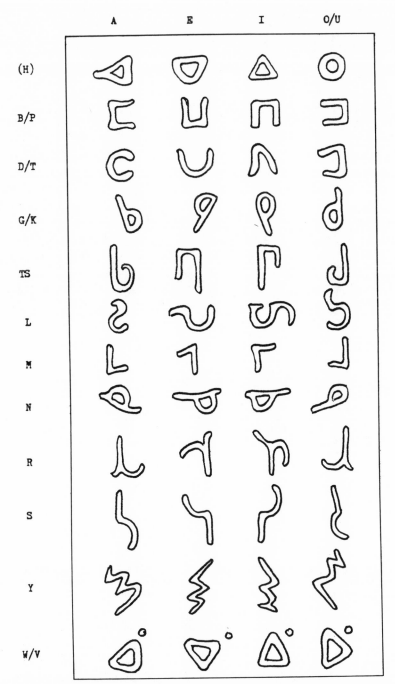

Figure 6-10. Syllabary found on ancient Basque inscriptions of Spain and Portugal, undeciphered until 1979, when I noted the match with the Algonquian syllabary of Canada and was able to give phonetic renderings of the ancient Iberian inscriptions. That these are indeed written in an early form of Basque language was confirmed (1980, 1981) by Imanol Agiŕe, the Basque epigrapher, lexicographer, and authority on the history of the alphabets of the world.

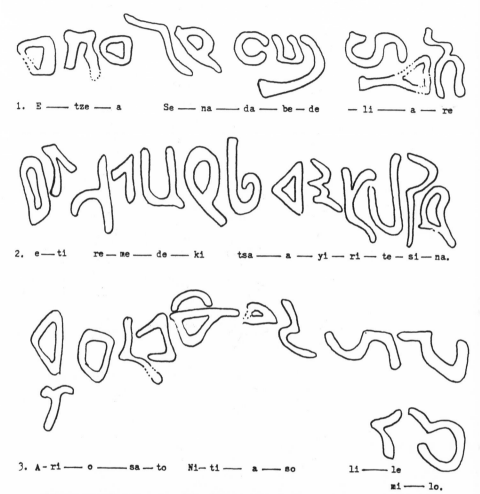

1. E —— tze —— a   Se — na —— da — be — de   — li —— a — re

2. e — ti   re — me —— de — ki   tsa —— a — yi — ri — te — si — na.

3. A- ri —— o ———— sa — to   Ni— ti —— a —— so   li —— le

mi —— lo.

Figure 6-11. *Decipherment of the first three lines of San Telmo stele,* an example of the Iberian texts, undecipherable until the match between the letters and the signs of the Algonquian syllabary was noticed in 1979. The translation reads:

1. House of the Apothecary
2. And of remedies for illnesses
3. Buy from me herbal medicines.

This inscription, now in the San Telmo Musuem, is one of the last known uses of the script in Spain, dating from medieval times. Other examples range back to the Bronze Age.

aning	Basque		Algonquian		
	guzki	ᑯᐢᑭ	gisis	ᑭᓯᐢ	Ojibwa
			gischuch	ᑭᐢᒍᐨ	Delaware
r	šita	ᓯᑕ	skwita	ᐢᐠᐎᑕ	Natick
t	alphorra	ᐊᕑᐳᓗ	awan	ᐊᐘᐣ	Ojibwa
v or fine rain	babada	ᐸᐸᑕ	papad-	ᐸᐸᑕ	Natick
udy weather	gohin	ᑯᐦᐃᐣ	guhn	ᑯᐣ	Natick
ad	aize	ᐊᐃᓭ	aiowastin	ᐊᐃᐘᐧᐢᑎᐣ	Cree
	aitše	ᐊᐃᒉ	outšou	ᐅᐟᒋ	Abenaki
	ulauza	ᐅᓚᐅᓴ	lutin	ᓗᑎᐣ	Old Algonquian
	etc.		etc.		
ter	uds*	ᐅᐨ	utan (-quench)	ᐅᑕᐣ	Natick
wash	kusi	ᑯᓯ	kusit (-flow)	ᑯᓯᐟ	Natick
wash	babi	ᐸᐱ	papen- (-drip)	ᐸᐯᐣ	Natick
nk	ziba	ᓯᐸ	sipe (-water)	ᓯᐯ	universal
er	šipa	ᓯᐸ	sipu (river, etc.)	ᓯᐳ	universal
od ce er aters	ibai	ᐃᐸᐃ	(n)ipe	ᐃᐯ	universal
	ibaiak	ᐃᐸᔭᐠ	ipog	ᐃᐳᐠ	
ean confluence of waters")	ur-keta	ᐅᕐᑫᑕ	kehta	ᑫᑕ	universal
nd	uts	ᐅᐨ	uto	ᐅᑐ	Natick
			wuto	ᐅᐧᑐ	Natick

dim. ustinta)

Table 3.

This comparative table, taken from my 1979 paper on the decipherment of ancient Basque, shows also that the language of the Algonquian Indians contains words of Basque origin. The last two columns compare the related pairs of words as written in the Cree-Basque syllabary.

scription cut on Woden-lithi's site shows, the actions of the Nordic colonists were of interest to the Algonquians, and an inscription in a language similar to Ojibwa, using the Basque (and therefore the Cree-Ojibwa) syllabary, makes reference to Woden-lithi's departure by ship. As already noted, Woden-lithi's relations with the Algonquians appear to have been cordial, and he refers as a "foreign friend" to one whom he has carved.

The beliefs and practices referred to in this chapter, worship of the sun and moon and worship of animals, appear all to derive from the Stone Ages and were doubtless a direct carryover from the late Neolithic.

But the Indo-European farmers who occupied Scandinavia toward the close of the Stone Age, and who are believed by Scandinavian archaeologists to be the direct ancestors of Bronze Age peoples in Scandinavia, were practical country people who perceived the sun as a supreme deity on whom the fertility of their crops depended, since only by planting seed at times determined by the position of the sun in the constellations could they be assured of success in reaping a harvest.

For their more personal needs they apparently evolved a whole pantheon of lesser deities. As the Bronze Age progressed, these lesser gods gradually assumed the role of major gods, and eventually the sun and the moon and the rest of nature were assigned by the priests to the lesser roles of servants of the new gods. For the Nordic peoples the leading members of the new pantheon were all sky gods. The new religion had already developed clearly defined roles for these gods, and in that capacity they accompanied Woden-lithi to America, as his presiding patrons.

7

THE GODS GO WEST—
WODEN AND LUG

Although both the Celts and the Nordic Teutons venerated the sun god above all others during the Bronze Age, the former calling him by the name Bel or Grian, the latter Sol or Sunu, each of these peoples recognized a host of lesser gods. These deities seem to have originated as spirits of nature, each in charge of particular natural manifestations, and later some of them were elevated to become major gods.

Thus Lug to the Celts was a god of light, who repelled the forces of darkness with his mighty spear. Much the same characteristics were apparently assigned by the Nordic people to Woden or Odin, who also owned a mighty spear and dealt destruction to the enemies of gods and men. Both Celts and Norse recognized a sky god who was named for thunder: Taranis in Celtic, Thunor or Thor in Nordic. Both had divinities in charge of war, of music, of writing skills and magic, and, especially, fertility, both male and female.

In America something happened that did not and could not happen in Europe. Relatively isolated and defenseless settlements of Celts and Nordic Teutons came into accidental and basically friendly contact. Inevitably there were intermarriages, and each side imparted its ideas to the other. Thus arose a peculiarly American blending of European concepts, which later permeated Amerindian thinking, as intermarriages became more extensive.

When the Celts crossed the Atlantic to settle in America they brought their gods with them. In the northeastern settlements, where native rock abounded, they built religious centers in the megalithic style. Some of the chambers still carry ogam inscriptions indicating the name of the god or goddess of the dedication (see Chapter 2, and Figure 12-14). In most cases the original inscriptions are now unreadable or totally effaced by time and weather. As centuries went by, and the Celtic people or their creole descendants dispersed across the continent, their concepts changed with the changing environment. In the Northeast the mother goddess was conceived as a female figure resembling the Punic Tanith, also as a nude image. On the prairies the mother goddess is represented as an Amerindian woman whose fringed clothes spell out in ogam her name and titles. Where there were no rocks, no stone chambers could be built, and they and the other megalithic structures all but vanish as we pass beyond the Great Lakes.

Chief of the Celtic gods was Lug, god of the sky and of light, and creator of the universe. His emblems are his spear and his slingshot. With the latter he once destroyed a one-eyed monster named Balar, who, with his sorcerer attendants the Fir-bolg, had gained the mastery of Ireland, Balar is depicted in an unlettered inscription on the Milk River, near Writing-on-Stone, Alberta. He is shown as having one leg and one arm, held aloft over his gigantic eye, which could kill hundreds merely by its glance. In this pictograph, Figure 7-2, Lug has just loosed the thong of his slingshot and the monster is about to bite the dust. Another and evidently much later depiction of Lug is that in Figure 7-1, where his name is given in Norse runes, one of many examples we now have of Norse influence on the western Celts in North America. Presumably the Norsemen came down from Hudson Bay to enter the prairie lands. In this petroglyph Lug is shown holding his magic spear, by means of which he defeats the forces of darkness each year, to usher in the returning spring. The last-mentioned petroglyph occurs on cliffs at Castle Gardens in Wyoming, and at the same site another Celtic god is identified by his name written in Norse runes. This is Mabona (or Mabo), the Celtic Apollo, god of music and of sports and the presiding divinity in charge of male fertility. In this context his symbol is the phallus, shown in the petroglyph on the rock above him.

The Punic traders of Iberia brought to America the coinage of Carthage and other Semitic cities, and these coins often depict a horse (the emblem of Carthage), or just its head and neck, or a Peg-

L —— U – G —— S

Figure 7-1. Lug, the Celtic god of light, is here identified in Norse runes of the period A.D. 750–1050. The name is in the possessive case: Lug's (site or his image). This remarkable petroglyph occurs at Castle Gardens near Moneta, in Wyoming, and the drawing is traced from a photograph taken by Ted C. Sowers of the Wyoming Archaeological Survey (1941). Although this is the work of an artist of relatively modern times, the theme harks back to the Bronze Age, as does the formalistic style, like that of the earliest Bronze Age.

asus with wings but without the rest of the animal's body. Since there were no horses in the Americas at that epoch, the Celts had vague and strange ideas as to what kind of animal it might be, apparently able to fly like a bird, yet resembling a deer in other respects. They sometimes carved representations of their gods or heroes riding on this magic animal of the skies, and often the hoofs are replaced by birds' feet. The body may resemble a boat, while the mane and tail provide the fringe ogam required to give a title to the composition. In this respect the American Celts copied exactly the conventions of the Celtic minters of Spain, forming the word C-B-L or G-B-L (for *capull,* horse), and in the case of a Pegasus, adding the suffix -*n* (-*ean,* meaning "flying"). Some of these flying heroes mounted on Pegasus-back may be intended for Norse Valkyries; others have the name Mabona or Mabo-Mabona incorporated in the ogam of the tail.

The god of knowledge, especially astronomy, astrology, and occult sciences, and of writing skills, was Ogmios. He is always represented as having a face like the sun, and sometimes he carries rods that spell G-M, the consonants of the word *ogam,* for Ogmios was credited with having given mankind the gift of ogam.

In later centuries, long after the time of Woden-lithi and his colonists, the descendants of the Nordic settlers began to migrate westward, to reach the Great Plains and, ultimately the West Coast from British Columbia southward to an undetermined distance. They also encountered other Amerindian tribes, especially the many Dakota tribes, usually now referred to as Sioux. With the passage of time these communities all blended, and so a part of the Nordic heritage was introduced into the Amerindian tradition.

While these events were occurring, a similar westward migration took place among the Celtiberian colonists who had originally occupied much of New England and also parts of the southeastern states. These Celtic migrants likewise reached the Plains, and they too blended with the Sioux tribes and the Shoshone. They also had a predominant influence in forming the Takhelne people of British Columbia. The Celts spread southward along the Pacific coast, through Oregon and much of California, where their ogam inscriptions are often to be found in excellent states of preservation.

Inevitably the two religious traditions, Norse on the one hand, Celtic on the other, both of them expressions of the original Indo-European pantheon, blended to produce a composite mythology. Thus we find Norse heroes depicted in what appear to be Celtic roles, and vice versa. These blended traditions persisted into modern times, and there were still artists painting ogam texts beneath Norse mythological subjects as late as the first decades of the nineteenth century.

All the foregoing inferences are attested to by the inscriptions. In localities such as the Milk River in Alberta, where inscriptions in ogam abound, the bedrock is so soft that the inscriptions cannot be many centuries old. Some declare their recency by incorporating depictions of Royal Canadian Mounted Police, or colonists with rifles—scattered incongruously among petroglyphs that depict the old Nordic gods and heroes.

It is clear that a tradition of sculpting replicas of still older petroglyphs must have persisted for thousands of years, and it is very probable that many of the artists whose work we now admire and whose ogam texts we can still recognize may not themselves have really understood what it was that they had been trained to sculpt. Perhaps, like the Egyptian carvers of Roman times, they merely knew that they were repeating old and hallowed texts from their remote ancestors, the meaning no longer known to them.

Whether this was so or not, the Amerindians have disclosed little of what lies behind their traditional art, or have cloaked it behind a disguise of later-invented myths. And as for the inscriptions, many of those that are still readable as ancient ogam cannot possibly have been cut in ancient times. They represent a fossil art, preserved intact from another age. We can be grateful to those artists who thus preserved the remote past for us in this way.

King Woden-lithi gives a concise summary of his pantheon of gods, which (like Snorri's *Edda*) he separates into the Aesir or sky gods and the Wanir or earth gods.

Chief of Nordic sky gods is Woden of the great spear Gungnir and, as stated above, he has much the same characteristics as Lug of the Gaelic Celts and Lew of the Brythonic Celts. He presides over magic and owns a magic ring that Loki, his son, had made for him.

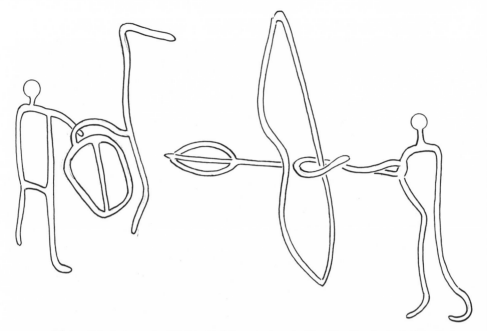

Figure 7-2. Lug, god of light (right), prepares to fire his slingshot at the giant (closed) eye of the one-legged monster, Balar, who is attended by one of the Firbolg. *Alberta Provincial Park.*

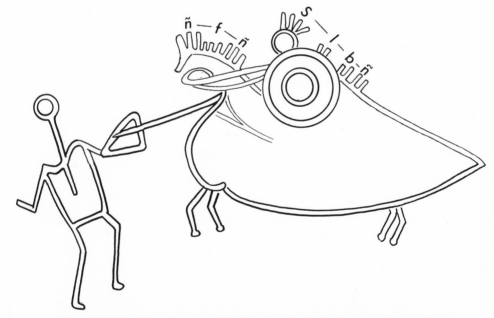

Figure 7-3. The fringe ogam on this depiction of a flying horse reads in a close approximation to Old Norse *Nefni Sleipnir*, "Its name is Sleipnir." The reference is to the magic steed Sleipnir, obtained by Loki for Woden. This is another example of the astonishing persistence of an artistic and mythological tradition, for the carving is in a nonresistant rock in the Milk River valley, Alberta, and must have been executed within recent centuries.

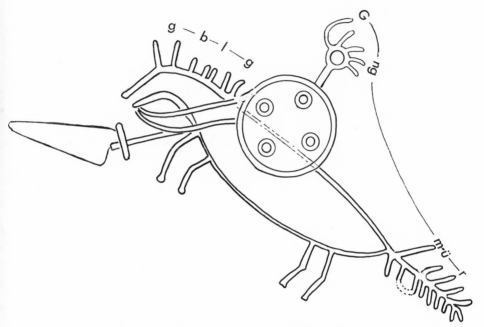

Figure 7-4. Ogam-inscribed flying horse of Woden, with a slightly garbled version of Old Norse words *Garflak Gungnir,* "The spear Gungnir." This, like many other inscriptions found along the valley of the Milk River, Alberta, is work carried out in recent centuries, and shows an astonishing retention of ancient tradition among peoples who now speak an Amerindian tongue and who had probably long since forgotten the meaning or pronunciation of the words incorporated into the rebus.

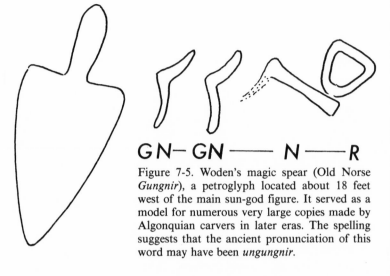

GN–GN —— N —— R

Figure 7-5. Woden's magic spear (Old Norse *Gungnir*), a petroglyph located about 18 feet west of the main sun-god figure. It served as a model for numerous very large copies made by Algonquian carvers in later eras. The spelling suggests that the ancient pronunciation of this word may have been *ungungnir*.

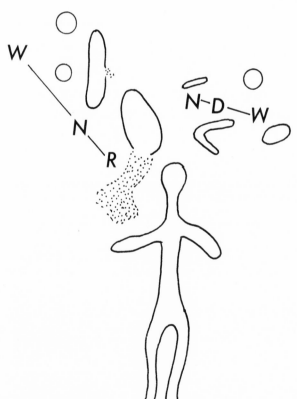

To the right of the Gungnir petroglyph is this image of Woden. It is lettered W-N-R W-D-N (Old Norse *Vanir Odin*).

The word *Vanir*, here rendered as *Wanir*, means earth gods and refers to some images cut nearby but not included in this diagram. The word *Woden* relates to the tall figure of the sky god shown here.

His magic spear is carved many times at Peterborough, some of the larger versions being perhaps the work of Algonquians copying from smaller originals. In one example (Figure 7-5), located about 18 feet west of the main sun figure, the letters GN-GN-N-R are written: *Gnugnir,* the Ontario version of *Gungnir,* by which name Odin's spear was known to the Vikings of a later age. These and other inscriptions show that the mythology of Odin in Viking times is fundamentally just a more elaborate development of the mythology of the Nordic peoples generally in the much earlier era of King Woden-lithi.

Woden himself is depicted as a male figure just to the right of Gungnir (Figure 7-5). His name is written W-D-N, Woden, in the English and Germanic form of his name.

About 14 feet south of the main sun figure another of Woden's possessions is depicted (Figure 7-10). This is a peculiar forked tree, identified as W-GH D-R-S-I-L, Ughdrasil, matching the world-tree of the Vikings, called Yggdrasil. The name is supposed to mean "Ugly Horse" and its link with the tree is obscure.

Woden was also regarded as the god who presided over the dead, with feasting and other pleasures of the flesh for warriors who died in battle. His assistants in bringing in the bodies of the slain, for restoration to life, were the Valkyries. I have not yet observed any reference to this mythology on the Peterborough site, but Figures 7-3 and 7-4 suggest that the myth of the Valkyries was imparted to the American Celts. The inscriptions depicting these strange riders of flying steeds were cut in nearly modern times by western plainsmen, probably Sioux, who had inherited the Celtic-Norse tradition.

The World

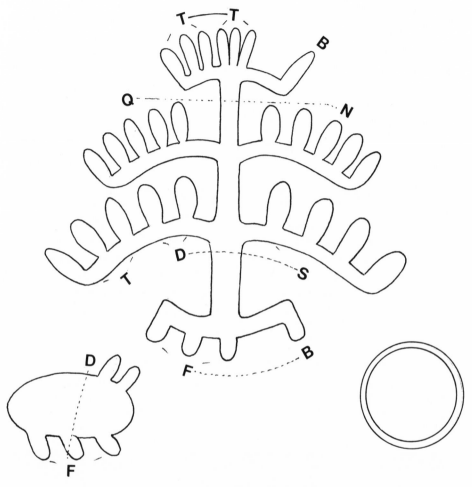

Example of Dyad Tree Ogam

F-D, Fad = dimensions   of the globe

T-T B Q-N T D-S F-B
Tuath bi ceann, ta deas fo.
North is set at the top, south below.

Figure 7-6. Evidently influenced by Norse fellow settlers in the west, the American Celt combined the mystical concept of the world-tree Yggdrasil with a scientific understanding that the earth is in fact a globe.

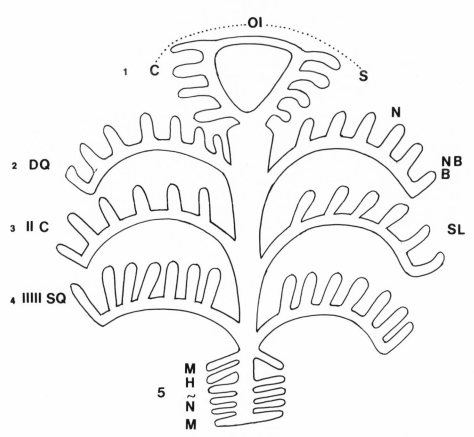

Figure 7-7.
Left side, left-hand ogam;   right side, right-hand ogam

1. S-OI-CH   There are seven
2. Q-D N-B (Caide neabi) Spheres in the sky.
3. I I Cé S-L (suile)   Two are for the eyes of the world,
4. I I I I I S-Q (seac)   Five for the wanderers (planets),
5. M-H-N-M (Mion ma)   The lesser-ones, surrounding them.

This appears to be the tree Yggdrasil.

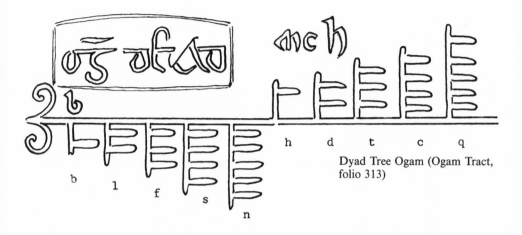

h   d   t   c   q

Dyad Tree Ogam (Ogam Tract, folio 313)

b   l   f   s   n

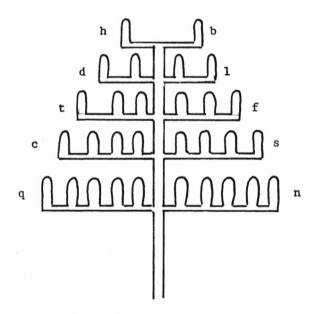

h   b

d   l

t   f

c   s

q   n

Figure 7-8. When written vertically, dyad ogam forms a tree-shaped figure, in which the left-hand branches carry the signs of the h-series (left-hand finger ogam), and the right-hand branches take the signs of the b-series (right-hand finger ogam). This style, evidently of high antiquity, appears on coinage of the Thracian Celts and is especially conspicuous in the Takhelne inscriptions of British Columbia. The upper diagram is taken from the Book of Ballymote, and is identified to the left by the scribe in Middle Irish Script as "ogam dyad."

Site Iny-7A   Site Iny-281

OGMA   GRIAN   AINEAĊ

Figure 7-9. The Gaulish god Ogmios, who presided over the occult sciences and was the reputed inventor of ogam writing, appears in Irish mythology as *Ogma grian aineac*, Ogma the sun-faced. Petroglyphs depicting the sun-faced god occur in California and Nevada, representing him with an ogam symbol that spells his name in ogam consaine script, held in his left hand, and a druid's wand, held in the right hand. These, together with much else in American Celtic inscriptions, stress in Irish affinity of the early Celtic settlers in America. *Maturango Museum and University of California, my interpretation.*

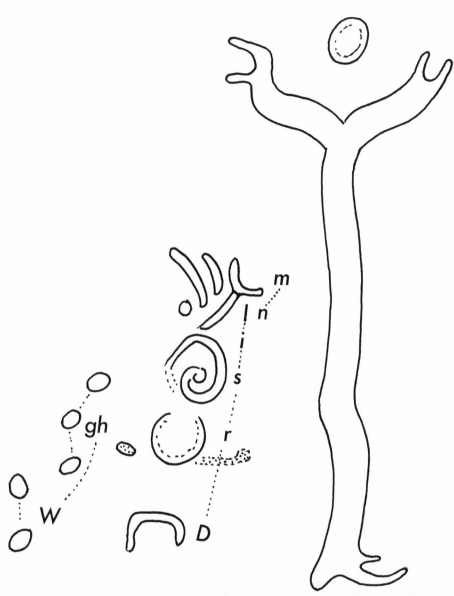

Figure 7-10. The Tree of Dread, Yggdrasil. At the command of Woden, Loki created a magic tree to support the world. It is here depicted as having only two branches, and is named W-GH D-R-S-I-L N-M (Old Norse *ugha drasil nama*, supposedly meaning "fearsome horse," rendered also *Yggdrasil*). The significance of the name is obscure. In Celtic versions the tree is shown with branches at successive levels, supporting the various regions of the heavens, the earth, and the underworld. This petroglyph lies 12 feet south of the main sun-god figure.

8
LOKI THE CRAFTY

One of Woden's sons was the crafty Loki of Viking tradition. He may well have been venerated more highly in Woden-lithi's time, not as a crafty ill-natured character, but as a skillful craftsman, for in the early Bronze Age technical skills would be rare and highly valued. About 10 feet north of the main sun figure at Peterborough there is an illustration of a galloping animal, and beneath it an ithyphallic figure (Figure 8-1), with the following text engraved:

M-GN L-M-S L-K L-A W-N W-V-GH W-D-N

(*magna lumis Loki lae wan Vighhya Slehefnir Wodena*) "By sorcery, cunning and venom Loki won the steed Sleipnir for Woden." The word *Slehefnir* is assumed to be the damaged section that lies beneath, to the right.

Loki was credited by the Vikings with having powers of persuasion that the skillful dwarves of the Mid-Earth could not resist. Whenever Odin needed something from the dwarves' factories, Loki was always sent to wheedle it out of them. Similarly, when Thunor, the thunder god, required a weapon to defend the Aesir, it was Loki who was sent for, and who found means of providing it. King Woden-lithi's text states that a dwarf manufactured the magic hammer named Mjolnir for Loki to give to Thunor. This inscription is given as Figure 1 of Chapter 10.

Loki, despite his malevolence, was a skillful craftsman himself, and seems in this aspect to represent the blacksmith god of the Greeks (Hephaistos) and the Romans (Vulcan). The Celtic equivalent of the latter two deities was Goibhnui and he, like the Graeco-Roman craftsman god, was lame. If, therefore, we equate Loki with Goibhnui (Figure 8-2), despite their apparent differences in tem-

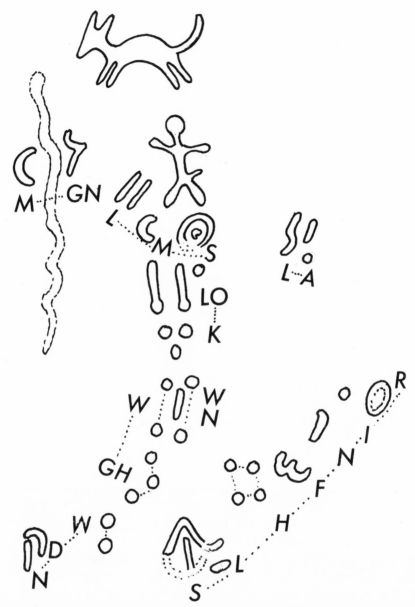

Figure 8-1. Loki used sorcery and serpent venom in overcoming adversaries and in carrying out orders from Woden. In this text, located 10 feet north of the main sun-god figure, he acquires by these means a magic steed called Slehefnir for Woden. (In the Norse version he creates a steed named Sleipnir for Odin.) The present text may be read as *Magna lumis lae Loki wan wigha Slehefnir Wodina*, matching similar Old Norse words that mean "By sorcery, cunning and venom Loki won the steed Sleipnir for Woden." The determinatives for horse and man (or male god) appear at the top and relate to the two proper names in the text.

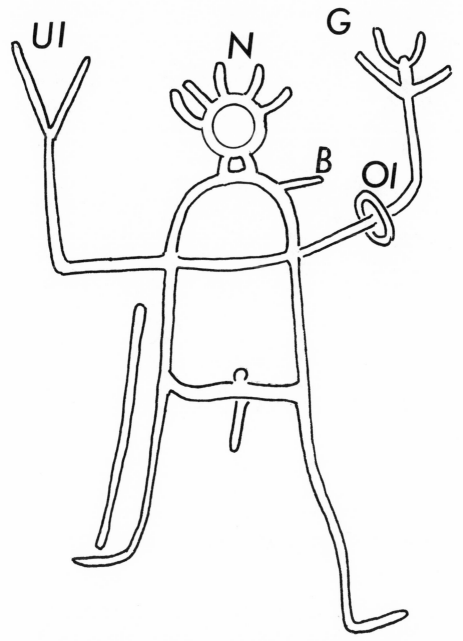

Figure 8-2. The Celtic god Goibhnui in this Milk River inscription from southern Alberta here declares his identity by deft finger ogam. Goibhnui was originally a blacksmith god, adopted probably from the Roman pantheon, for he is lame, like Vulcan and Hephaistos, the blacksmiths of Roman and Greek mythology. In America he seems to have taken on a new role as the tutelary god of farmers. American Celts depict him as having the right leg shorter than the left, and he uses a walking stick.

perament, we should perhaps include here the activities presided over by Goibhnui in his new roles in America. For, as the Celtic settlers moved westward, they encountered the Rocky Mountain bighorn sheep, and began to harvest its wool by means of annual roundups, Goibhnui now became the presiding genius over the craft of farming. Once the wool was shorn, it passed under the aegis of the mother goddess.

At suitable locations in the mountainous areas of the far west the Celts hunted the bighorn and the antelope. In Nevada, however, and also in British Columbia, there was an annual round-up by shepherds, on foot. The pictographs show them carrying shepherds' crooks (Figure 8-3). It is probable that the long drystone walls noted by Professors Robert F. Heizer and Martin A. Baumhoff (1962) were to facilitate driving the wild sheep into a confined area, where they were shorn of wool. The various pictographs (Figures 8-4, 8-5, 8-6, 8-7, 8-8), some of them rebus ogam, depict sheep, and also other animals. The spinning of yarn and various parts of the vertical loom and its associated tools (shed battens, loom-comb [replacing a reed], and frame) are shown in pictographs given in chapter 12. The methods appear to be the same as those used by the present-day Navaho. In Nevada I was told of persistent legends that the region was formerly in the possession of a now-vanished people called "sheep-eaters." The technical farmer's words appearing on some of the inscriptions are in some cases of Norse origin. This fact, taken with the mixed Celtic-Norse features of some of the mythological inscriptions and the occasional use of Norse runes, can only mean that a contact occurred between the Celts of the Milk River (and also of Wyoming) and Norse visitors or settlers.

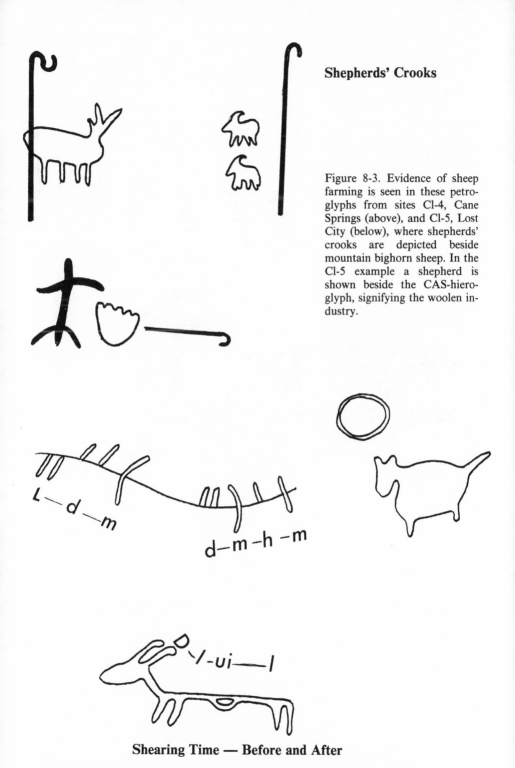

Shepherds' Crooks

Figure 8-3. Evidence of sheep farming is seen in these petroglyphs from sites Cl-4, Cane Springs (above), and Cl-5, Lost City (below), where shepherds' crooks are depicted beside mountain bighorn sheep. In the Cl-5 example a shepherd is shown beside the CAS-hieroglyph, signifying the woolen industry.

L — d — m

d — m – h – m

ϊ - ui — l

Shearing Time — Before and After

Figure 8-4. Above: At John Corner's site 6, Stein River, in British Columbia the ogam may be read as *Leadb deimhe am* "A fleece timely to be sheared." Below: A rebus in which the parts of the sheep's body read *Deall olla*: "Robbed of wool." Site 99 of Corner near Towdystan, British Columbia.

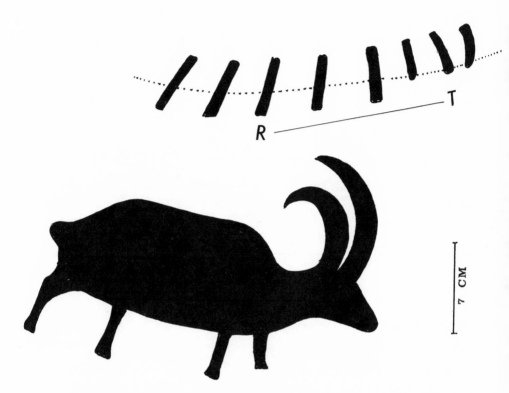

Figure 8-5. Valley of Fire, Atlatl Rock, Nevada, University of California site Cl-l, ogam script, Gaelic language, Decipherment: *R-T* (Old Irish *rete*), a ram. The species depicted is Rocky Mountain sheep, or bighorn, first recorded in modern times by Lewis and Clark, but well known to the ancient Celts.

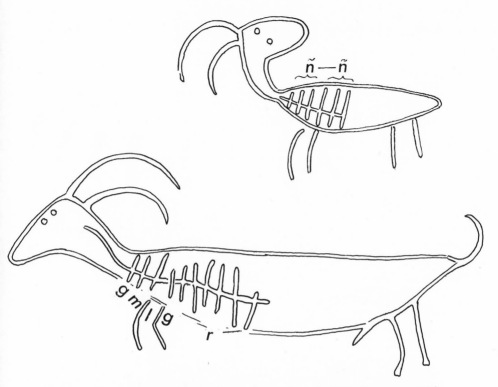

Figure 8-6. Sheep depicted in rebus form at sites along the Milk River, near Writing-on-Stone, southern Alberta. Above: *nan*, "little one." Below: *gemlingr* (a Norse loan word), "hogget ram" (a two-tooth yearling). Here and elsewhere in the West there is evidence of Norse-Celtic contacts.

Figure 8-7. Antelope rebus from the Milk River, Alberta. There was no native European animal corresponding to this species, so the American Celts invented the name seen here, *da-gheagham*, literally "two-prong."

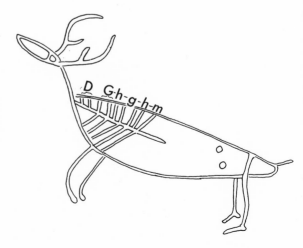

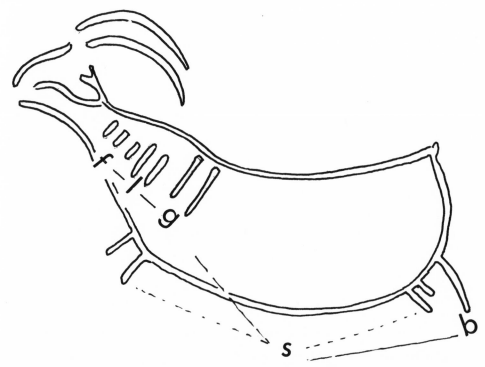

Figure 8-8. Evidence of Norse-Celtic contact along the Milk River sites, Alberta, is apparent in this rebus where the ogam letters read *felags-bu*, a Norse term applied to farm stock that was owned in common by a local community.

9

TSIW MIGHTY-IN-BATTLE

In Anglo-Saxon and Norse mythology Tiw is the son of Woden (Odin) and therefore a member of the superior sky gods, though subservient to Woden. Two striking differences are evident in the mythology of King Woden-lithi, which antedates the historical era from which Anglo-Saxon and Norse mythology derives.

First, the name of Tiw is rendered in the ancient German manner, with an initial *ts*-sound (*z* of Old High German), and so, like Thunor, Tsiw reminds us of the southern Teutons rather than of the Norsemen.

Second, his image is by far the largest of the gods' after the sun god and the moon goddess. He is also shown as the tutelary deity of ships. The ship depicted beside his main image is not a warship, however, but a trading vessel, with a deep capacious hull for cargo and without the banks of oars of a naval ship. It may well be Woden-lithi's own ship.

By tradition Tiw was the god of battle, and he presumably had that department of human aggression under his charge in Woden-lithi's day also. His major image lies some 30 feet west of the main sun figure at the Peterborough site (Figure 9-1). He is shown as a stoutly built man, standing on the initial letter TS of his own name, his right hand held aloft, his left arm with the hand severed, the stump dripping blood. To his upper left stand the letters of his title L-M-Y-TH, "maimed" (Old Norse *lamidhr*). Beside him to his right lies the giant wolf Wenri (Fenrir of Norse mythology). According to Snorri, who wrote in the twelfth century, Fenrir was one of the evil progeny of Loki. He became a menace to the gods, and Odin ordered him to be haltered. Only Tiw was willing to attempt

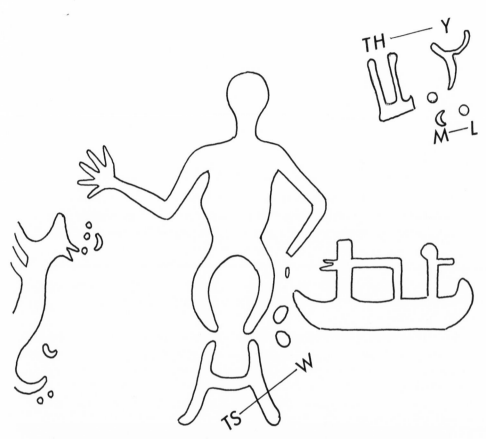

Figure 9-1. Tsiw (Tiw of Anglo-Saxon lore), depicted as the major god of the Aesir, protector of ships, god of war, protector of the sky gods, for whose sake he sacrificed his left hand to the giant wolf Wenri (left). His title here is given as *Tsiw lymth*, "Tsiw Maimed." The inscribed dedication by Woden-lithi occurs beneath this figure, and is given separately in Figure 9-2.

the task, and to achieve it he had to pacify the wolf by placing his hand in its mouth, as an earnest that the halter would not in reality restrict him. When the truth appeared otherwise, Fenrir bit off Tiw's arm. Obviously this myth was already established in the early Bronze Age, since it is so clearly depicted here.

According to philologists, Tiw is the same god as the Greek Zeus. The Old High German name Tsiwaz, like the name by which Woden-lithi knew him, resembles Zeus. His tasks included that of holding up the sky. This he is shown doing in an unlabeled pre-maiming situation in a petroglyph (Figure 9-3) located 6 feet west of the main sun figure.

In his role as a war god Tsiw has as one of his symbols a battle-ax. In my book *Saga America* I recorded two iron battle-axes that had been discovered in America, though they seem to be of Viking origin. One was found at Cold Harbour, Nova Scotia, and the other (Figure 9-4) at Rocky Neck, on the Massachusetts coast. They were formerly owned by William Goodwin, who first protected Mystery Hill, and they are now in the Goodwin Collection in the Wadsworth Atheneum in Hartford, Connecticut.

At the time when I prepared the text for *Saga America* (1980) I had not realized that the Tifinag alphabet is of Nordic origin, and consequently I was baffled by what appeared to be Norse axes engraved, as these two are, with Tifinag letters. Not expecting the alphabet to render Norse language, I could find no Libyan match for the words the letters seemed to spell, and was forced to record them in the book with the comment (*Saga America,* page 352), "The markings are letters of the Tifinag alphabet of Libya, although the axes appear to be Viking."

Now that we can expect Norse language written in the Tifinag alphabet, the decipherment is clear, and we can be sure that the ax is indeed Norse. The inscription shows that axes of this type were awarded as marks of honor by Norse kings, and that even though they are products of the Iron Age, they retain the ancient Tifinag as a persistent tradition from ancient times, as do many royal gifts given in modern times. The inscription may be transcribed as L-A-N S-M E-K-M M-M S-M E-L, to be understood as *Lae sami ekjum emum, sami eli,* "Royal award for the honor of battle widows, and for the honor of old age." That two such awards have

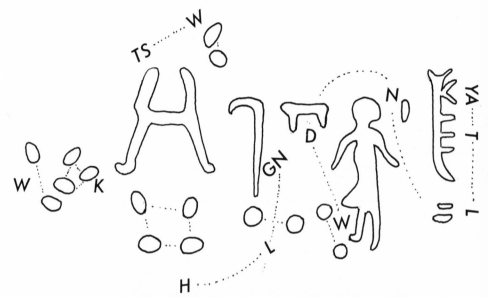

Figure 9-2. King Woden-lithi's dedication inscribed immediately below the image of the war god Tsiw. The text reads from left to right and, by supplying the vowels, may be pronounced as *Wik halgen Tsiwa Woden-litya,* "The image hallowed to Tsiw by Woden-lithi." The last two letters of the king's name are given as ogam in a ship rebus. This is also a common feature of inscriptions at Bronze Age sites in Sweden, where prayers for the safety of ships are rendered in ogam letters that are fitted together to make diagrammatic pictures of ships. This inscription is discussed in the text, where the connections of the words with modern English and other Teutonic tongues is explained.

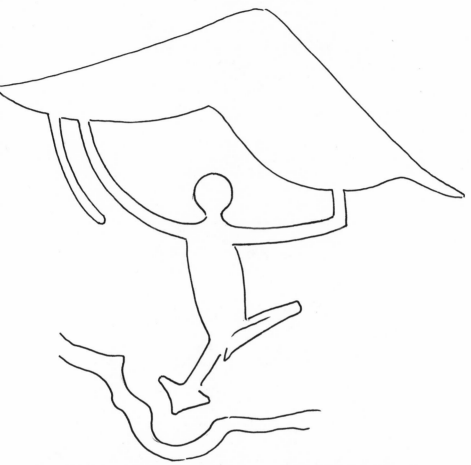

Figure 9-3. A Bronze-Age conception of celestial mechanics. The god Tsiw holds up the canopy of the roof of heaven, standing upon Walhol (Valhalla). This unlabeled figure lies 6 feet west of the main sun figure at the Peterborough site. Beneath Tsiw, in a part of the inscription shown in Chapter 13, the Aesir are ascending to Walhol as the onslaught of the monsters of Middle Earth initiates the Twilight of the Gods.

Figure 9-4. Norse iron battle-axe found at Rocky Neck, near Gloucester, on the Massachusetts coast, now in the Goodwin Collection, Wadsworth Atheneum, Hartford, Connecticut. The Tifinag inscription (see text) shows that it was a royal award given to battle veterans and widows of warriors killed in battle. *Photo Malcolm D. Pearson.*

been discovered in North America, and none (so far as I can learn) in the Scandinavian countries themselves seems surprising.

Woden-lithi associates Tsiw with ships, as his dedicatory inscription shows, and this must indicate that at the epoch when Woden-lithi lived, the god was regarded as a tutelary deity for sailors. Since the king was himself a sailor, it is natural for him to have given such prominence to his patron, greater than that which he accorded to Woden or any of the other gods, save only the sun god. I have been unable to find, so far, any other references to Tsiw on American rocks, nor indeed to find which god was regarded as in charge of fishing. For want of information on the subject, I include here, as perhaps the proper place, some of the inscriptions that relate to ships and to fisheries (Figures 9-5, 9-6, 9-7, 9-8, 9-9). Most of these are demonstrably Celtic in origin, some are unidentified, and merely depict ships of the Bronze Age type.

The illustrations have detailed captions. However, it should be explained that Celtic custom, still to be found in Ireland within living memory, required that the local chief of any community be granted a tax comprising one tenth part of all catches of fish. The tithe was used by the chief for the support, not only of his own family, but of indigent families or widows and fatherless children. (The American gypsies, at least in the Northeast, still maintain a similar custom, or did so up to ten years ago when I was collecting linguistic material from the Boston gypsies.)

The inscriptions that illustrate these fishing practices come from the Tule Lake region, on the border of Oregon and California. Although no fishing is now carried out there, the local Indians and museum authorities confirm that very great runs of fish used to occur in former times, and that they were indeed caught in nets, as the inscriptions state. It is also of great interest that the unit of measurement of fish by tally is called the M-S, to be read as Old Irish *maois,* the meaning of which is given in Patrick S. Dinneen's Irish-English, English-Irish dictionary (2nd ed., Dublin, 1927, p. 709) as "a hamper of 500 fishes." The lettering on the texts gives the remaining details. These texts are traced from photographs made at Tule Lake by Wayne and Betty Struble, who detected the ogam and brought the site to my attention.

b—d

Figure 9-5. Birds flying overhead spell out *B-D* (Old Irish *bat*, Welsh *bad*), a boat. Pictorial lessons in ogam found at Garfield Flat, Mineral County, Nevada.

Figure 9-6. Another pictograph of an archaic type of ship, found by John Corner at his site 86, Adams Lake, British Columbia.

Celtiberian Site, East Peninsula, Tule Lake

D-EA- Ň ——— S-G——UI ——— R   M   M—UI————— R ——— G

Dean-sguir
A tally made
            ma
            for
    Muirig
    the chief

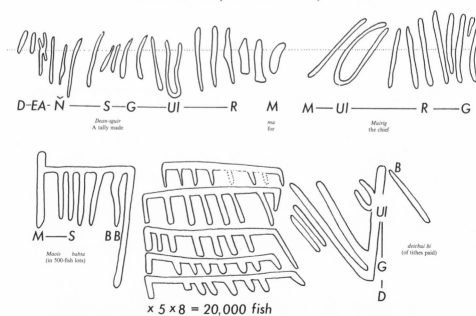

M — S   B B

Maois   babta
(in 500-fish lots)

B
UI
G
I
D

deichui bi
(of tithes paid)

x 5 x 8 = 20,000 fish

Figure 9-7. "A tally made for the chief of tithes paid in *maois* lots each of 500 fish." Ancient Celtiberian inscription cut in lava rock at Tule Lake, California, East Peninsula petroglyph site.

Celtiberian Site, East Peninsula, Tule Lake

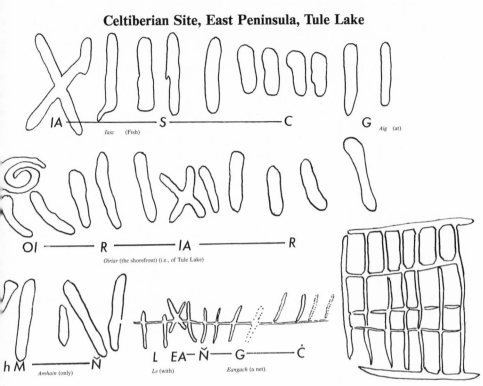

IA ———————— S ———————— C   G   *Aig* (at)

Iasc (Fish)

OI ——— R ——— IA ——— R

Oiriar (the shorefront) (i.e., of Tule Lake)

h M ———————— Ň   L EA– Ň — G ———— Ċ

Amhain (only)   *Le* (with)   *Eangach* (a net).

Figure 9-8.

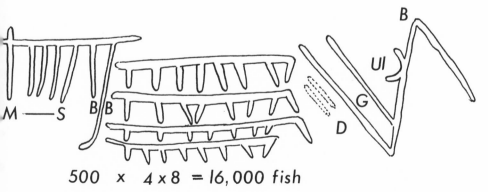

M — S   B/B   D   UI   B   G

500   x   4 x 8 = 16,000 fish

Figure 9-9. Another example of a tithing record, Celtiberian site, Tule Lake, California. Decipherment as for previous example. The number of fish caught is 160,000.

10
THUNOR THE THUNDERER

Third of the sons of Woden, and fourth of the Aesir gods, we may note Thunor (*Thor* of the Norsemen). The form of his name suggests a north German rather than Scandinavian affinity for Woden-lithi's tongue.

Thunor was the name by which he was known to the Anglo-Saxons, before the Vikings came to England. He is accorded much space on Woden-lithi's rock platform, and seems to have been one of the major objects of veneration. About 24 feet south-southwest of the main sun figure he is depicted (Figure 10-1) with his sword and hammer, but no text. He wears a high-peaked conical helmet. Some 20 feet west of the main sun figure his famous hammer is depicted, together with its personal name, M-O-L-N-R (*Mjolnir*). In the Bronze Age all famous weapons had personal names, on the model of Siegfried's sword, Volsung. Images of the short-handled hammer, usually not labeled, are seen all over the site. About 11 feet southeast of the main sun figure Thunor himself is depicted (Figure 10-2), helmetless, arms akimbo, his hammer beside him to the right, and its name, M-L-N-R, inscribed to the left. In a corrupt spelling M-N-R the hammer appears about 45 feet to the south-southeast of the main sun figure, beside a pair of serpents, and to the right Thunor stands, demonstrating his mighty glove, one of the sources of his power. As conqueror of the sea giant Ymir (Himir of the Norsemen), he may have been accorded special veneration by Woden-lithi's mariners.

He is shown with his high conical helmet and his hammer also in a petroglyph composition (Figure 10-5) centered at about 15 feet northeast of the main sun figure. This shows Thunor at the out-

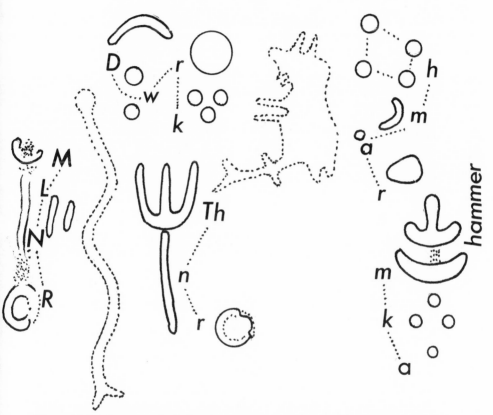

Figure 10-1. Thunor, god of thunder, owned several powerful weapons, one of which was his hammer, Mjolnir, always represented as having a very short handle. This inscription, about 10 feet southwest of the main sun-god figure in Peterborough, is one of several similar ones at the site. It reads M-L-N-R D-W-R-K H-M-A-R M-K TH-N-R, "Mjolnir: a dwarf made Thunor strong by [this] hammer." The hieroglyph *hammer* appears below the word H-M-A-R.

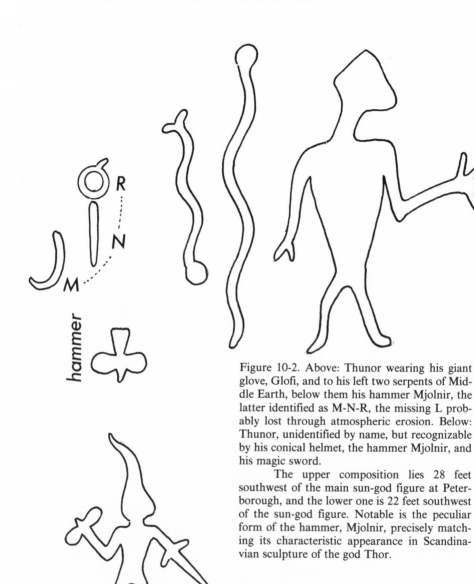

hammer

Figure 10-2. Above: Thunor wearing his giant glove, Glofi, and to his left two serpents of Middle Earth, below them his hammer Mjolnir, the latter identified as M-N-R, the missing L probably lost through atmospheric erosion. Below: Thunor, unidentified by name, but recognizable by his conical helmet, the hammer Mjolnir, and his magic sword.

The upper composition lies 28 feet southwest of the main sun-god figure at Peterborough, and the lower one is 22 feet southwest of the sun-god figure. Notable is the peculiar form of the hammer, Mjolnir, precisely matching its characteristic appearance in Scandinavian sculpture of the god Thor.

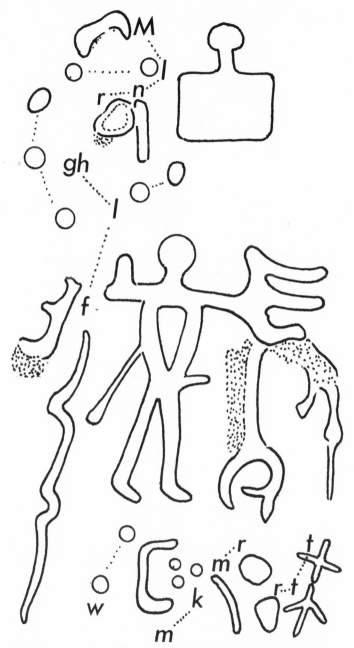

Figure 10-3. The power of Thunor over the Serpents of Midgard was increased by his hammer, Mjolnir, and his giant glove, Glofi. This inscription, which lies about 9 feet southwest of the main sun-god figure, depicts the god strangling the serpents. The text reads:

M-L-N-R GH-L-F W M-K R-M R-T-T (Old Norse *Mjolnir, Glofi, ve maki orm rittit*: The hammer Mjolnir, and the glove Glofi; woe is their power to the serpent, writhing).

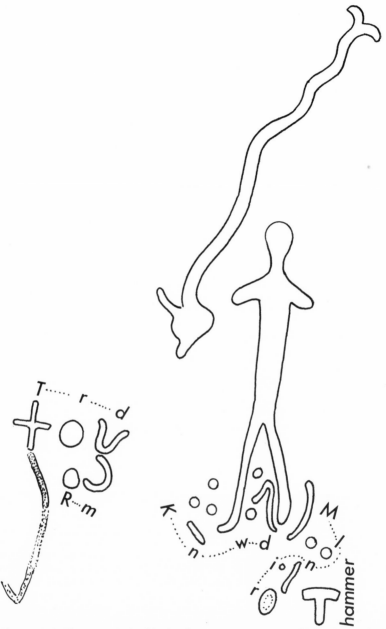

Figure 10-4. Thunor's duel with the Orm, serpent-dragon of Middle Earth. The text reads M-L-N-R K-N-W-D T-R-D R-M (Old Norse *Mjolnir knudh, traudh Orm*, "Mjolnir has struck, the Serpent-dragon weakens"). This inscription lies 18 feet north of the main sun-god figure, at the Peterborough site. Thunor's hammer, Mjolnir, is depicted beside its name, to the lower right. More details on the monsters of Middle Earth and Jotunheim are given in Chapter 13.

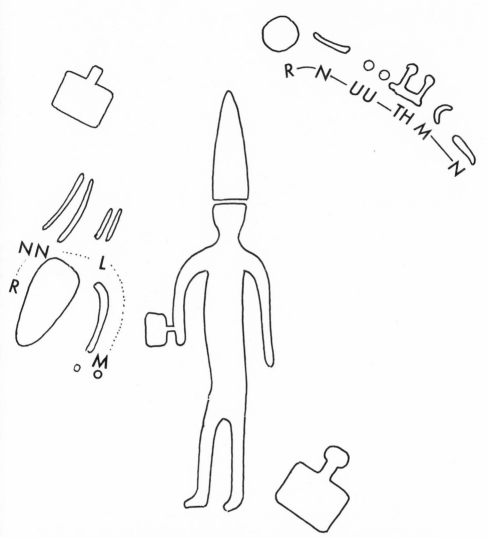

Figure 10-5. This Peterborough inscription, depicting the Thunderer, reads from right to left: *Nema Thuunor Molnnir,* "Thunor grasps his hammer Mjolnir." The engraver of this petroglyph seems to have had a penchant for reduplicating letters, in the manner of the Pictish engravers of ogam in Scotland. The area depicted lies about 18 feet northeast-by-east of the main sun-god figure. Thor, the Scandinavian equivalent of Anglo-Saxon and German Thunor, is shown wearing a conical helmet in some Norse art, as for example a bronze figure now in the Reykjavik Museum. The short handle of the hammer is also typical of Norse versions, and is the subject of a special explanatory myth according to which Loki accidentally broke off a part of the original handle.

set of the final battle of the gods against the forces of the underworld. The giant serpent-dragon of Middle Earth lies to the right,
coiling its body, with a text composed of the dot-letters of the alphabet along its length. The text that accompanies this composition appears to be a continuation of the text given in Figure 10-1, where a
dwarf is recorded to have made Molnir for Thunor. This section
reads:

N-M TH-W-N-R M-L-N-R H-K R-M L-K-K L-W-K L H-W

which may be intepreted as *Nema Thunor molnir haka Orma likkja
luk la hawa,* "Thunor takes up Molnir to strike at the Serpent, its
body lying coiled in the sea." (In figure 10-5 only the god and his
hammer, and the first three words of the text are shown). The dragon defeated Thunor in the end, leading to the ascent to Walhol, as
recorded later in this section.

As we have already seen, the ogam alphabet that for so long
has been supposed to be an exclusively Celtic script was in fact well
known in Nordic countries as early as the Bronze Age. This fact accounts for the otherwise untranslatable ogam inscriptions that occur in the Western Plains and as far west as the valley of the Milk
River in Alberta, Canada.

Here occur many petroglyphs cut in soft bedrock; they are
obviously not more than a few centuries old at most. One such is
shown in Figure 10-6, where a supernatural figure is depicted holding aloft what appears to be a rake. Indeed, the archaeologists who
have recorded these and similar inscriptions say just that. Now it so
happens that the *Ogam Tract* written by the mediaeval Irish monks
describes a special kind of ogam called by them *ogam reic:* literally
"rake ogam." It is not known in Ireland as occurring in petroglyphs, nor indeed anywhere save in the manuscripts written by the
monks. Thus the American petroglyphs are the first examples to be
recognized as archaeological artifacts.

When first I was confronted with these examples I naturally
expected the language contained in the ogam script to be Celtic, and
a Celtic related to Irish Gaelic. But the decipherment proved baffling, as no Celtic words known to me matched the concatenation of
consonants present in the rakes and in the associated finger ogam
(also mentioned in the Irish texts).

Figure 10-6. Thunor with his hammer, Mjolnir. The script is *ogam raic* ("rake ogam"), but the language is Nordic, as the hammer and its name prove. The petroglyph is one of a large series along the Milk River, Alberta, Canada.

After the presence of Norse or Nordic inscriptions was made clear by the Peterborough texts, the solution of the mysterious rake ogam of the Milk River petroglyphs became evident. The letters are indeed ogam, but the language is Nordic, allied to Old Norse. As can be seen from Figure 10-6, the "rake" represents the hammer Mjolnir and the god depicted is Thunor, here rendered as ogam T-N-R.

As god of war the deity may be presumed to rule over the art of using weapons, whether for battle or for hunting. Figure 10-7 is an example of many similar petroglyphs, in this case written in Celtic language, where hunting scenes are portrayed. It is from Site 77 near Canal Flats in British Columbia, discovered by John Corner. This is modern work, for the medium in which it is executed is paint, exposed to the atmosphere; another piece of evidence pointing to the long memory of the Amerindians. The artist was a member of the Takhelne tribe, with a spoken tongue of partly Celtic derivation.

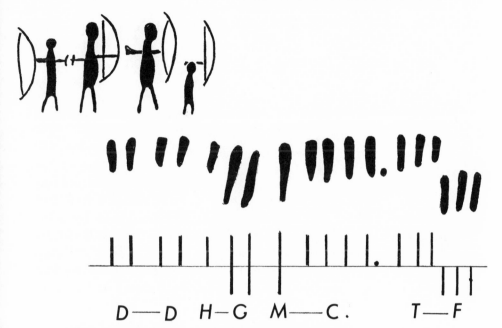

Figure 10-7. Decipherment of script ogam, Gaelic language.

D-D (Irish *daidi*) fathers
H-G (Irish *og*) and
M-C (Irish *maca*) sons
T-F (Irish *tafain*) hunt

Translation: "Fathers and sons. The hunt."

These roots point to Irish, not Scots, Gaelic. Note the punctuation point.

11
MABONA AND FREYR—
THE PHALLIC GODS

King Woden-lithi seems to have devoted less space on his platform to the Wanir, gods of the earth, than to the other deities. Under the inscribed word W-R-Y-aR (*Freyar*) he has depicted a phallic god 11 feet west of the main sun figure. Beside Freyr is an up-ended ship, one of his symbols by Norse tradition, though the connection with male fertility is not immediately obvious. The hull of a ship is perhaps here regarded as a phallic symbol.

The interesting interconnection between Celtic and Nordic gods, already noted in Figure 7-1, under Lug, is again evident in a petroglyph at Coral Gardens, near Moneta, Wyoming, photographed by Ted Sowers of the Wyoming Archaeological Survey. The Celtic god Mabona is shown below his symbol, a giant phallus, and beneath is written his name, in younger runes. Again we have evidence of a later contact between the American Celts and Norsemen of the period of Leif Eriksson.

Much more obvious attention is given to the worship of the power of the phallus as a fertilizer not only of women but of Mother Earth herself, in the shape of the great stone phallic monuments that the Celtic and Nordic peoples erected in Europe and that their American cousins placed at corresponding suitable sites in the New World. That these are, in some cases at least, Bronze Age monuments is evidenced by the presence of ogam consaine script, making reference to ancient pagan divinities and rituals. Figures 11-4 through 11–12 illustrate typical examples in both Europe and America; I have discussed the inferred fertility rituals in *America B.C.*

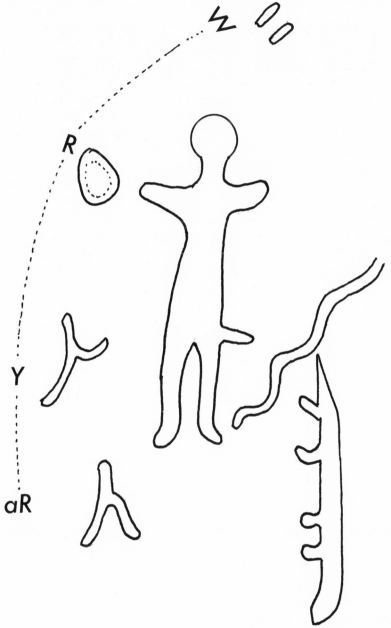

Figure 11-1. About 12 feet west of the main sun-god figure at Peterborough, there is a representation of W-R-Y-aR (Old Norse *Freyr*), the male fertility god, together with his symbol, a ship upended as a phallic monument. The god himself is depicted as ithyphallic.

That Mabo was preferred by the youth of America to his Norse equivalent Freyar is made clear by the much larger number of inscriptions dedicated to the former, and usually written in Celtic ogam of the type called fringe ogam (see Introduction, Figure I-1). A telling piece of evidence is seen at Woden-lithi's site (Figure 11-3), where the male fertility god is named in ogam as Mabo. And the reason for the preference of youth for the Celtic god of youth is his three spheres of activity—sex, sports, and music—all of primary interest to the youth of every country.

In his first aspect, that of god of male sexuality, the numerous stone phalluses and menhirs, erect or fallen, in both Europe and North America, bear silent witness. Figures 11-4 through 11-6 show three European examples in France and Spain, and North American examples appear in Figures 11-7 through 11-10. Most of the American phalluses have fallen into a recumbent posture. Those on Phallus Hill, South Woodstock, Vermont, have since been transferred to the museum of Castleton State College in Vermont.

In New England, groups of phallic stones were erected on the summits of hills (Figure 11-12). Whether these were used as calendar determination sites is not yet established.

In British Columbia and in the Nevada and Californian deserts, there occur inscriptions in ogam, in a Celtic language, relating to matings and the marriage bond (Figures 11-13 and 11-14).

In addition to the worship of Mabo as a fertility god, interest in the various games and athletic sports under the protection of Mabo, and brought by ancient colonists from Europe is manifest in various petroglyphs (Figures 11-15 to 11-18). What may be the Celtic ball game of *camanachd* seems to be depicted in some cases. Running and hurling the caber are other athletic subjects, and we know from historic contacts in the nineteenth century that the Takhelne tribe of British Columbia practiced a sport much resembling the Scottish caber-tossing. An inscription at Cane Springs, in Clark County, Nevada, recorded by Professors Robert Heizer and Martin Baumhof, carries fringe ogam that implies that the game depicted can scarcely be separated from baseball, the latter an invention attributed to New York State in modern times.

The third aspect that Mabo assumes, as the Apollo of the Celts, is that of the god of music. This is succinctly referred to in a

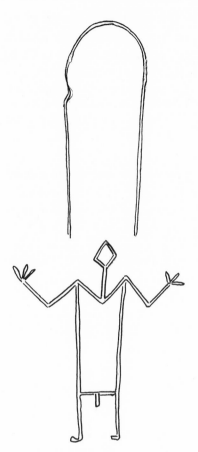

Figure 11-2. Celtic god of the phallus, Mabona, depicted with his name inscribed in runes. This is another of the Coral Gardens petroglyphs showing Norse contact in Wyoming. Traced from a photograph by Ted C. Sowers of the Wyoming Archaeological Survey.

M – B – N

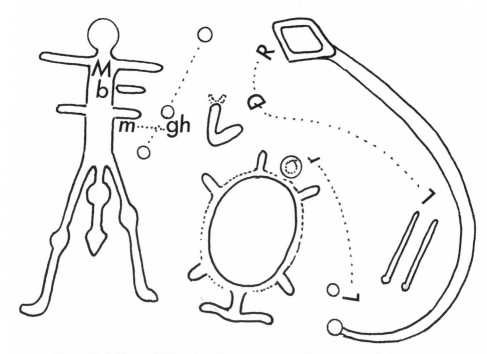

Figure 11-3. Norse-Celtic cultural contacts recurred many times in North America, but in this inscription from Woden-lithi's Peterborough site we seem to have the earliest known example. Mabo is identified in ogam as a Celtic divine youth (using one Tifinag letter, *gh*), and his attributes the phallus and the turtle-shell lyre appear, together with the Nordic equivalent symbol of music, the great curved lur trumpet of Bronze Age times, still used in the Viking era 2,000 years later. This remarkable evidence of cross-cultural influences in the Bronze Age is located about 30 feet north of the main sun-god figure. The inscription reads: M-B M-GH L-R L-D-R (Old Norse *Mabo maegi, lir, ludhr*: "Mabo of the youth, lyre, and lur." A small lizardlike figure, probably an Algonquian addition, has been omitted from the diagram.

Figure 11-4. Phallic megalith or menhir, Spain. *Photo Professor Leonel Ribeira.*

Figure 11-5. Phallic menhir at Kerouezel, Brittany. *Joseph Dechelette.*

Figure 11-6. Giant phallus of Kerdef, Brittany. *Joseph Dechelette.*

Figure 11-7. Phallic menhir photographed at the time of its discovery on the top of what was then named Phallus Hill, South Woodstock, Vermont. This, like others, has since been transported to the Castleton College Museum, Castleton Vermont. *Photo Peter J. Garfall.*

Figure 11-8. Another of the phallic stones found on Phallus Hill by John Williams and the author in the years 1974 and 1975. *Photo Peter J. Garfall.*

Figure 11-9. Large fallen phallus found in central Vermont. *Photo Joseph D. Germano.*

Figure 11-10. Details of the partly eroded ogam consaine inscription on the phallus shown in Figure 11-9. The ogam letters apparently refer to ceremonies held at Midsummer (Beltane). *Photo Joseph D. Germano.*

Figure 11-11. Fallen inscribed phallus, one of a series found by John Williams and the author during the 1975 season, near South Woodstock, Vermont. The ogam text apparently refers to fecundity of the mother goddess Byanu. The language on all these New England phallic ogam inscriptions is Celtic. *Photo Peter J. Garfall.*

Figure 11-12. Groups of phallic menhirs occur on hilltops in New England. This assemblage, in New Hampshire, provides a match for those found near South Woodstock, Vermont. *Photo Byron Dix.*

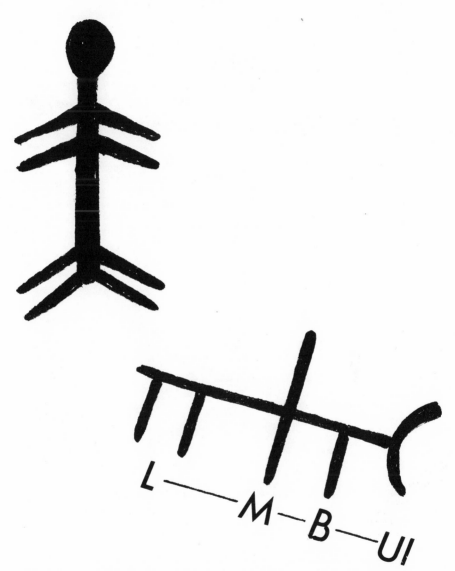

Figure 11-13. Pictographs in British Columbia, of relatively recent date, discovered at his Site 2, Chandler Ranch, near Lillooet, by John Corner, relate to matings and marriages. Decipherment: L-M-B-UI (Early Irish *lanamain*, Scots Gaelic *lanain*, "copulating)." Similar pictographs record ancient Nordic wedding ceremonies.

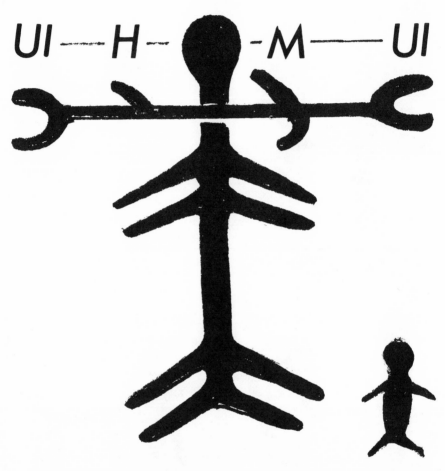

Figure 11-14. Also from John Corner's Site 2 is this pictograph recording a wedding ceremony. Decipherment: UI-H-M-UI (Irish *ughaim*, "yoke" or "harness," Welsh *iau*, "a yoke," Cornish *iou*, etc.) "the marriage bond." Ogam script in rebus form, to simulate a yoke, Celtic dialect.

Figure 11-15. *Camanachd* player? Petroglyph in black basalt, site Ch-71, Stillwater Range, Churchill County, Nevada. About 14 inches high. *Heizer and Baumhoff*.

Figure 11-16. Hurling the caber, a Celtic pastime. These two petroglyphs are from University of California site Ly-1, East Walker River, Nevada, and were originally recorded by Professors Heizer and Baumhoff.

TaFaiN = RUNNING

Figure 11-17. Runners, with Gaelic ogam inscription, from John Corner's Site 68, Vernon, British Columbia.

Figure 11-18. The ball game in ancient Nevada, as depicted at Cane Springs, site CL-4 of the University of California numbering. T-L (Gaelic *tilg*, "pitch"); B-L (Gaelic *buail*, "bat"); G-B (Gaelic *gab*, "catch"); R (Gaelic *ruaidh*, "runs," none registered on the scoreboard). Two teams (Gaelic D C-S-N, *Da cuisean*) are mentioned but not named.

Figure 11-19. Mabo here combines the aspect of phallic god and god of music, his head lyre-shaped, his body phallus-shaped, while his arms and penis spell the name Mabo (M-B) in ogam consaine. John Corner's Site 65, Vernon, British Columbia. The pictograph is a recent work by a Takhelne speaker of a mixed (creolinized) Celtic-Amerind tongue.

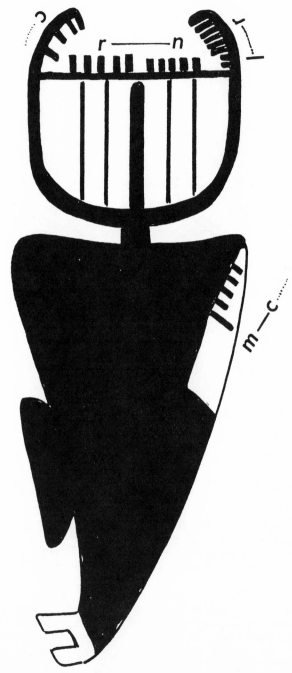

Figure 11-20. The two faces of Mabo the Melodious, Apollo of the American Celts and god of music. In this aspect, depicted at Heizer and Baumhoff's site Cl-4, Cane Springs, Clark County, Nevada, he is lyre-faced. The ogam lettering reads in consonantal Gaelic R-N C-L-R-C-M (Irish *rann claruicim*) "I sing stanzas to music."

Figure 11-21. The two faces of Mabo the Melodious. In this second aspect, also depicted at site Cl-4, Cane Springs, his Gaulish (and usual American) name Mabo forms his face, and his ogam hair spells the word C-T (Gaelic *cetan*), the name of his festival on May Day. He wears the antlers of a deer god. On his right arm appear ogam letters spelling *cetan*. In his left hand he carries a palm frond whose ogamic leaflets spell his title B-N-N-H (Gaelic *binn*), the Melodious. His right hand holds the disk of the returning sun, after winter.

Takhelne pictograph (Figure 11-19) discovered by John Corner near Robson, in British Columbia at his Site 65, where the god has the head of a lyre, while his outstretched arms make the letter *m,* and his erected phallus an ogam *b,* thus spelling his name.

The lyre-faced god appears in various inscriptions in Nevada (Figures 11-20 to 11-22), with remarkable fringe ogam inscriptions incorporated into the petroglyphs as rebus forms. The captions to the figures give details. Designs evidently influenced by these compositions enter into the art of the Navajo and Apache tribes, who entered the western territories as late inwanderers from eastern Siberia (their language still retains many recognizable Turkmenian roots). As I proposed in *Saga America,* it seems likely that these late invaders dispossessed the Pueblo peoples and acquired many of their art forms, so that the Navajo and Apache today are regarded as the foremost exponents of Amerindian culture in North America. In the process they seem to have acquired the Mabo rebus and converted it into a new but similar style, expressing a wholly different tribal mythology from that of the Celts from whom these figures originated.

Dancing to music, the dancers holding stag's antlers, is an ancient Celtic cultural feature, also reflected in the North American petroglyphs (Figure 11-23).

Amerindian musicians possessed many different though simple types of musical instruments. But the petroglyphs depict a wider range than was found in recent times and, in addition to the lyre, we see various representations of the Celtic harp, both the large and the smaller kinds. The associated ogam lettering, in a Gaelic language, is illustrated in Figures 11-24 to 11-25, and the captions explain this. Competitive performances on these instruments may have been judged by priests (druids), ensconced in seats like the curious stone ones that occur in New England (see Figure 11-26).

The conclusion we reach, then, is that Norse and Celtic colonists in ancient time, even as early as Woden-lithi's epoch, came to North America and influenced one another and the Amerindian neighbors they encountered, producing a rich culture with varied strands. The inability of the Norse people to establish bronze industrial sites in America led to the disappearance of the great trumpets, the lurs, but the various instruments manufactured from turtle shell and wood, such as the lyre and the harp, were capable of manufacture here, and so survived almost to modern times.

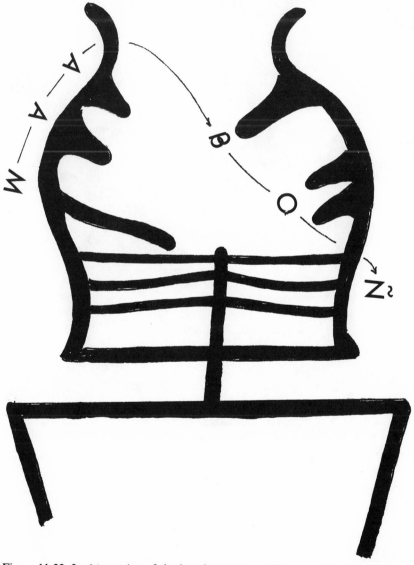

Figure 11-22. In this version of the lyre-faced god, at Heizer and Baumhoff's site Wh-13, White Pine County, in eastern Nevada, the ogam strokes on the cusps of the lyre include vowels, and his name is given as M-A-A-B-O-Ñ, the three strings of the lyre providing the termonal nasal Ñ.

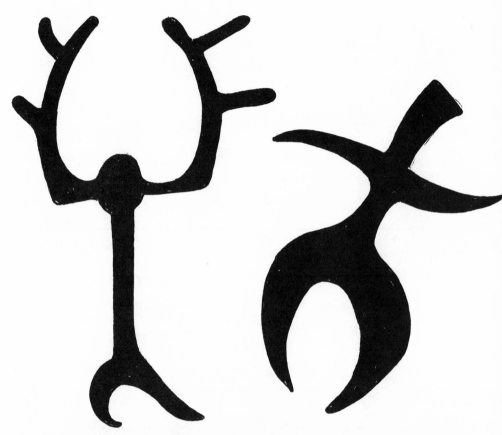

Figure 11-23. Morris dancers, petroglyphs in black basalt, Heizer and Baumhoff's site Ch-71, Stillwater Range, Nevada; the two dancers are on separate boulders.

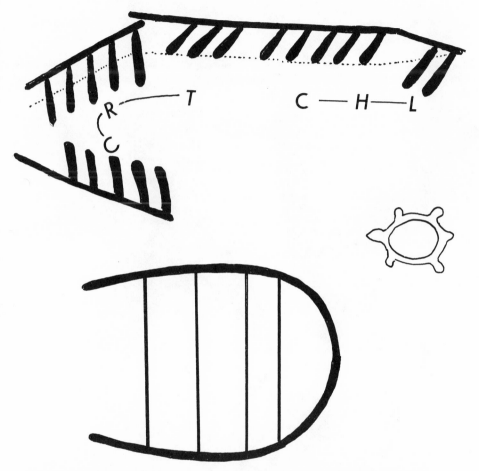

Figure 11-24. The lesser Celtic harp. At Site Wa-5, Spanish Springs, Nevada, the inscription and pictograph are both engraved on the same rock, side by side. Decipherment: C-R-T C-H-L (Gaelic *cruit chiuil*), the lyre or lesser harp. This term for the harp appears to be Scots rather than Irish Gaelic. The unusually complete ogam consaine text is 18 inches in length, the harp about one foot across. Inset to right, pictograph (drawn to a different scale) of a tortoise shell at Site Cl-145, such as might have provided the sound box, as in the case of Greek lyres.

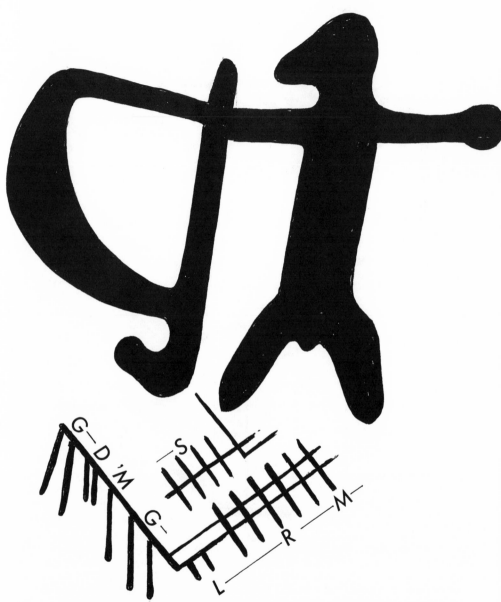

Figure 11-25. Song accompanied by the harp, Site Ly-1, East Walker River, Neva-da. The harpist is depicted on stone g, the inscription on adjacent stone e; G-D 'M G-L-R-M-S (Gaelic *gota 'm clarsac*), "song accompanied by harp."

Figure 11-26. At various localities in New England, since the matter was first made known in *America B.C.* (1976), remarkable massive stone seats or "druids' chairs" have been discovered. One of the best examples was found while excavating for backfilling for a house at Sutton, west of Boston, Massachusetts. *Photo Malcolm Pearson.*

12
THE MOTHER GODDESS

The mother goddess is depicted by the Celts in America and their Amerind descendants as a divine being with a celestial grace, whether she be shown as a young woman or as an elderly grandmother figure. The Norse, on the other hand, depict the terrifying aspects of worship of the goddess, in which a priestess with elaborate ritual becomes her voice and announces mysterious instructions. The concept of a divine mother seems to be the most ancient religious belief, for the Paleolithic peoples left behind them images and paintings of pregnant females, apparently expressing the wonder and the importance of fertility to the maintenance of the band or tribe. Later, when the essential preliminary role of the male in fertilizing the female was understood, the religion seems to have changed toward a father-god orientation, and the divine couple bred numerous divine progeny, each of whom became responsible for one or another of the fundamental human activities and interests.

Figure 12-1 shows one of the Milk River inscriptions at Writing-on-Stone, near Coutts, in Southern Alberta, where fringe ogam identifies the female figure as "Byanu, Mother of the Gods, Queen of the World," the language being Celtic. Figure 12-2, by way of contrast, from the same region, shows a Norse version of the goddess, seen in the guise of her priestess, as graceless and repulsive as the Celtic version is attractive.

The megalithic symbols of the mother goddess in America are the same that she has in Europe—the *Men-a-tol* or female stone, literally "stone-with-a-hole." Figure 12-3 shows a men-a-tol at Land's End in Cornwall, England, and Figure 12-4 a New England equivalent found and photographed by Hulley M. Swan at Jeffer-

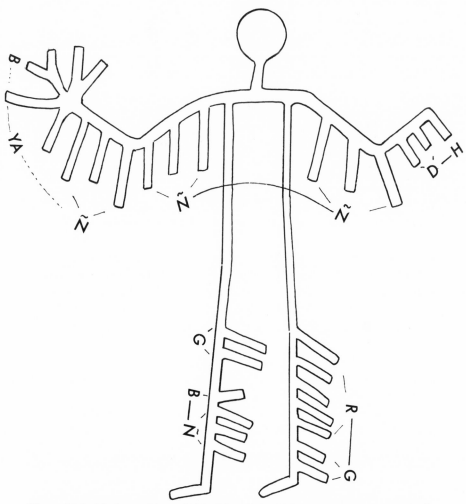

Figure 12-1. Mother-goddess of the Celts of the Plains. Decipherment: B-YA-Ñ Ñ-Ñ D-H, G B-Ñ-R-G (*Byanu, Nana Dhe, Ge Banrigh*) "Byanu, Mother of Gods, Queen of the World."

Figure 12-2. *Mal Freya gad* (reading *g* for *k*), "Freya gives utterance: the spiked staff." The priestess of Freya served as her medium and, when conducting divination, wore a special headdress and carried a special staff. This petroglyph at the Milk River site in Canada evidently depicts a divination ceremony.

Figure 12-3. Men-a-tol at Land's End, Cornwall, England. *Photo Donald L. Cyr.*

Figure 12-4. Men-a-tol at Jefferson, New Hampshire. *Photo Hulley M. Swan.*

son, New Hampshire. The precise significance of these "holey-stones" in Europe has been debated. In modern times engaged or newly married couples exchange kisses through the aperture, and babies are passed through the hole to bring good luck. These may be ancient practices.

The sun, and his celestial manifestation as a sun god, was always appealed to for warmth and rain to promote growth of crops. But so also was Byanu, the Celtic mother goddess, as an inscription at Tule Lake, California, shows (Figure 12-5). It was photographed by Wayne and Betty Struble. Other gods were also invoked. An inscribed stone placed in an ancient plantation in New York and found by John H. Bradner, invokes both Byanu and her divine son, Mabo. Thunor, in his later transformation into a rain god, was invoked by the Dakotas and Mandans. Plowing was virtually impossible in North America, for lack of suitable draft animals. Thus we are perhaps to interpret Woden-lithi's inscriptions of what appear to be plowmen (Figure 12-6) as no more than a didactic reference to Scandinavian practices. A Danish version of an early Bronze Age plowman is shown in that same figure.

When the Celts traveled west and discovered the Rocky Mountain bighorn sheep, they established a sheep-farming industry based on stock running wild, but rounded up (on foot) once a year for shearing (see Chapter 8). The product of this farming industry was, of course, raw wool. This, in turn, became the basis of a spinning and weaving industry, and the inscriptions in Nevada indicate that the mother goddess—or *a* mother goddess—was considered the tutelary deity of such activities. In the guise of a female that looks like the Celtic Sulis, we find inscriptions in Nevada dedicated to some female diviniity (Figures 12-7a, 12-7b).

The rocks of the Nevada plateau are rich in their petrographic commentary on the activities of these early farmers and wool-workers. At one site we find depictions of needles and thread, each labeled in fringe ogam with the names of the tools in old Gaelic. We find pictures of embroidery stitches. One ingenious petroglyph at Lost City, Clark County, Nevada, is in effect an advertisement for the wool industry, showing the production of cloth from the sheep's back by means of a looped wool thread, with pendant threads that spell ogam letters (Figure 12-8). The various

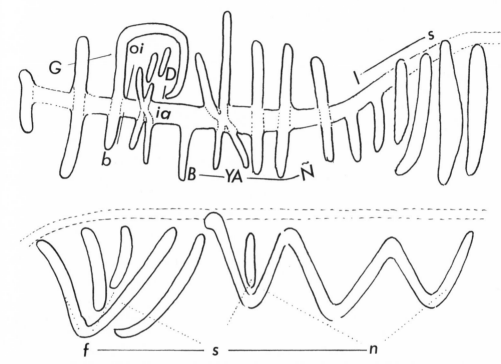

Figure 12-5. A prayer to the earth-mother, *Goib Dia Beanu leas fasan* ("Pray to Beanu that the corn may grow"). This inscription is cut in lava rock face, at a Celtiberian site at East Peninsula, Tule Lake, California. *Deciphered from a color photo by Wayne Struble.* It is a common feature at this site to find the separate staves of letters such as *n, c,* and *r* (which use 5 staves each) joined in a zigzag manner, as above. Scribes at this site also will transfer the arris above or below the characters if there is a long sequence of lower- or upper-case letters. In the example above the transition from a medial stem line to one that passes above the line is well shown. The word *dia* (goddess) seems to have been inserted as an afterthought, crammed into the *oi*, an unusual feature.

stages in converting the raw wool into yarn, then into a ball of yarn, including the carding, are all depicted (Figures 12-9 to 12-11). Setting up the warp on a frame is shown on Figure 12-9, and a vertical loom of the type afterward used by the Navajo appears in petroglyphs at Valley of Fire, Nevada (Figure 12-10). The various tools of the weaver, the battens, rods for weaving to cause the shed to alternate between throws of the shuttle, pegs, and loom combs (which replace the modern reed) all appear (Figure 12-11). And the final product, in this case a dress length, embroidered at the warp-ends (Figure 12-12), is shown.

Other and equally important information comes from the burial goods deposited with the bodies of the dead at ancient burial places, such as those of the early Woodland Period investigated by members of the Archaeological Society of Tennessee at Snapps Bridge, near Kingsport. Here we find actual pieces of equipment, such as loom weights, inscribed with appropriate words in ogam or Iberic, in the Celtiberian or Basque languages, indicating the functions of the objects, which were evidently buried with their owners (see Chapter 15 for more details). These latter finds came to notice through the observations of Dr. William P. Grigsby, who first noticed what he correctly inferred to be writing on some of the artifacts in his large collection.

Similar artifacts are found in Britain, as for example at the Windmill Hill site, occupied by the late Neolithic builders of Stonehenge. These have been recorded and well illustrated, and it is plain to see that inscriptions similar to those in North America occur, even the identical words. And similar inscriptions to those found on amulets in graves are also found inscribed on the stone chambers of New England. Thus, an invocation to the goddess Byanu, the mother-goddess of this chapter, occurs on a Windmill Hill amulet, and a similar text was reported in 1976 in *America B.C.* from a stone chamber dedicated to Byanu at South Woodstock, Vermont.

On the ceiling of the same chamber at South Woodstock occurs a depiction of Byanu in her guise as Tanith, the mother goddess of the southern Iberians and of their Carthaginian neighbors (Figure 12-14).

Near the same site John Williams and I found in 1975 the torso of a fallen image of a female divinity, evidently Byanu, whose name appears in various local contexts (Figure 12-13).

These examples illustrate the continuing and widespread influence of the concept of a mother goddess in North America just as in Europe.

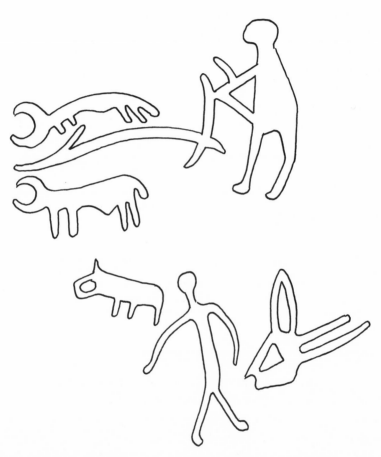

Figure 12-6. When Scandinavia was occupied at the end of the Neolithic period by farming people, the availability of draft animals in the shape of the native European oxen made plowing a possibility. The upper petroglyph, in Bronze Age style, is from Denmark. At Woden-lithi's site, some 40 feet north of the main sun-god figure, occur two compositions, one of which is shown below the Danish example. This Canadian petroglyph seems to indicate a plowman, though no draft animal was known in Canada. Since Woden-lithi's aim seems to have been to inform and instruct, perhaps this represents a Scandinavian scene and a suggestion that search be made in America for suitable animals.

Figure 12-7a. An unnamed goddess (probably Sulis, patron of the domestic arts) is here mounted upon a deer. She holds the hieroglyphic symbol of spinning and weaving, a bolt of cloth in the shape of a foot. *Cas* (a foot) is also the Gaelic verb "to spin thread." This unusual petroglyph occurs at site Cl-5, Lost City, Nevada, where many other references to the spinning and weaving art are to be seen.

Figure 12-7b. The goddess Sulis, patron of spinning and weaving, is here identified by the ogam rebus giving the letters of her name, and arranged to form the outline of a bighorn mountain sheep, her American cult animal. This petroglyph occurs at site Cl-123, in Keyhole Canyon, Nevada. Decipherment of the rebus: S-L-UI (Gaulish *Sulis*, or *Sulevia*), Athene (Minerva).

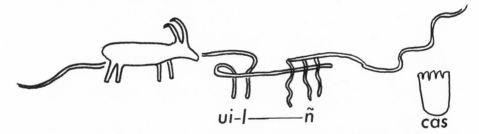

Figure 12-8. Symbols of the wool industry in Nevada, at site Cl-5, Lost City, southern Nevada, discovered by Professor Julian Steward in 1929, on the east bank of the Muddy River. Here a spun woolen thread loops about a bighorn sheep and then coils to form the ogam letters that spell "wool." Decipherment: UI-L-Ñ (Gaelic *olann*, Old Irish *oland*, Old Welsh *gulan*), "wool." The site is richly decorated with petroglyphs depicting sheep and shepherds and other aspects of the wool trade.

To the right is the hieroglyph *cas*, a foot, constantly found associated with inscriptions relating to spinning wool, because *cas* is also the verb *to spin* in Gaelic.

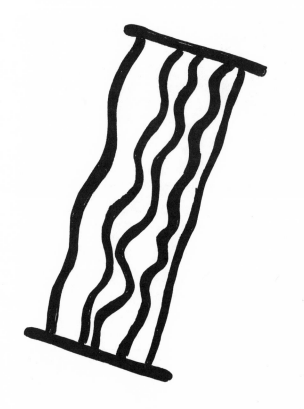

Figure 12-9. Weaving equipment, Cane Springs site, Cl-4, southern Nevada. Decipherment: F-UI (Gaelic *fuidne*, rods for weaving).

Ogam rebus depicting a ball of wool, Cane Springs, site Cl-4, Nevada. Decipherment: R-UI-G (Gaelic *ruigean*, "ball" or "roll of wool".)

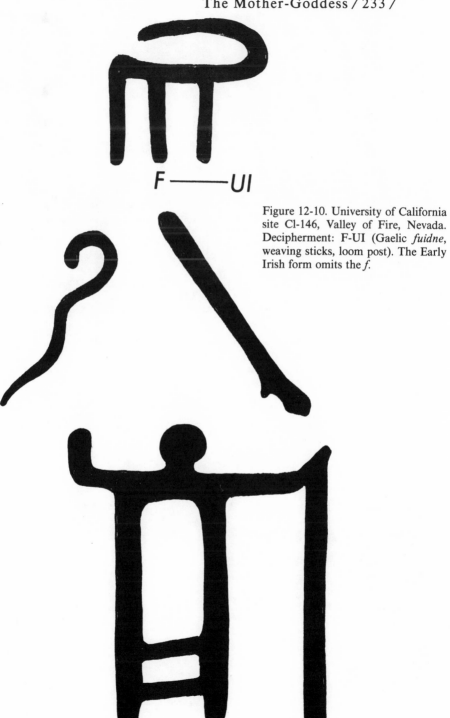

Figure 12-10. University of California site Cl-146, Valley of Fire, Nevada. Decipherment: F-UI (Gaelic *fuidne*, weaving sticks, loom post). The Early Irish form omits the *f.*

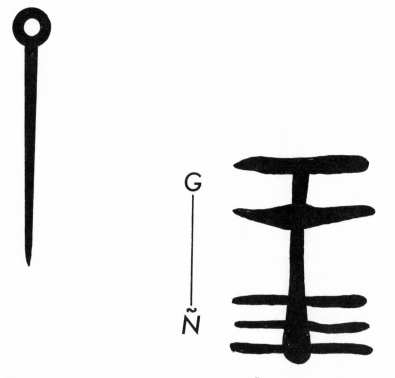

Figure 12-11. Weaving equipment. Decipherment: Ñ-G (Irish *cnag*, a pin or peg). Site Cl-145, Valley of Fire, Nevada.

Valley of Fire, site Cl-1, Nevada. Decipherment: G-R (Old Irish *cir*, "loom-comb").

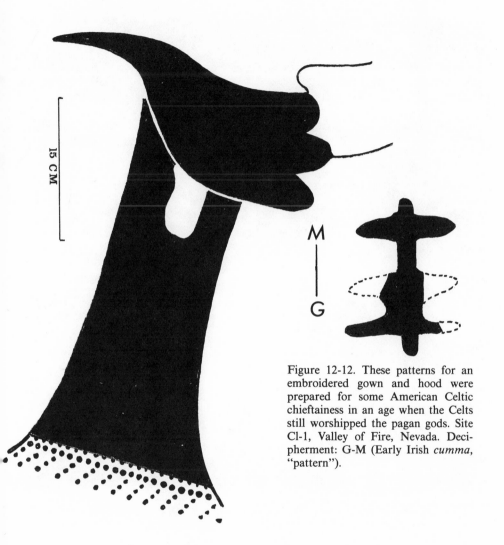

Figure 12-12. These patterns for an embroidered gown and hood were prepared for some American Celtic chieftainess in an age when the Celts still worshipped the pagan gods. Site Cl-1, Valley of Fire, Nevada. Decipherment: G-M (Early Irish *cumma*, "pattern").

Figure 12-13. Torso of a female stone image, believed to represent the mother goddess Byanu, found in 1975 by the author and John Williams near Woodstock, central Vermont.

Figure 12-14. Tanith-like figure of Byanu on the ceiling of the chamber at South Woodstock, Vermont, on which the name *Byanu* is inscribed in ogam consaine, matching the lettering of an amulet at Windmill Hill, England. *Photo Peter Garfall.*

13

GIANTS AND MONSTERS— TWILIGHT OF THE GODS

In Scandinavian mythology the underworld, Jotunheim, is inhabited by the evil progeny of Loki and by other giants and monsters. One of Loki's children was the giant wolf Fenrir, who became a menace to the gods, and had to be placed under restraint in a magic halter. None dared to capture the beast, however, until Tyr, the god of war, allowed the wolf to take his arm in his jaws as a guarantee that the halter would not restrain him. When Fenrir discovered that he had been tricked, he bit off Tyr's arm, so the god is depicted as maimed.

This ancient myth, as noted previously, is depicted on Woden-lithi's inscription in at least two places, Figures 9-1 and 9-2. About 21 feet from the main sun figure, slightly east of the north-south axis, occurs a wolf figure that is labeled L-Z F-N-R. The beast appears to be caught in some kind of trap. The inscription seems to mean "Fenri locked," assuming that L-Z is the root *laesa* in Old Norse, "to lock."

Another depiction is seen some 30 feet southwest-by-west of the main sun figure (Figure 13-1). It shows the wolf running free. It is lettered W-N-R M-L M-N-D. This evidently means "Wenri Crunch-Hand," the form *Wenri* being alternative to *Fenri* (*Fenrir* in Norse), *mel* being the verb to "crush" or "grind," and *mond* meaning "hand." The figure of the wolf is placed just to the left of the main image of the god Tsiw, whose left hand he has just bitten off. The god, with blood still dripping from the wound, stands defiantly, over the conspicuous dedication made by Woden-lithi (Figure 9-1).

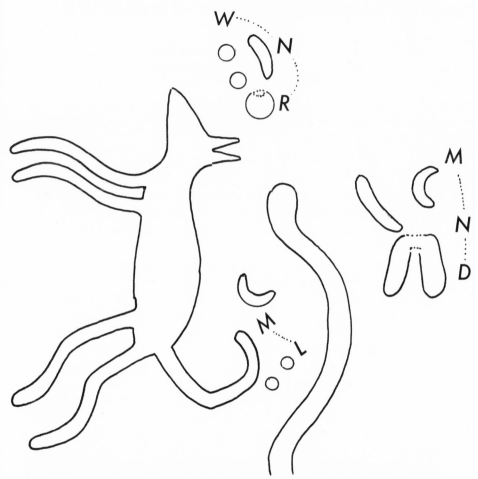

Figure 13-1. Wenri Crunch-Hand, the giant wolf that bites off the hand of the god Tsiw, is depicted in this petroglyph and inscription, placed just to the left of the image of the god, above Woden-lithi's dedicatory inscription. It is located about 30 feet southwest-by-west of the main sun god figure. The inscription is; W-N-R (*Wenri*, Old Norse *Fenrir*), the personal name of the giant wolf; M-L (*mel*, to grind or crunch) and M-N-D (Old Norse *mond*, a hand).

Two giants with similar names occur in Norse mythology. One of them, Ymir, is present at the creation of the earth, and his body is carved up to constitute the world. The other, Himir, is a sea monster who is defeated in battle with Thunor. The version presented by Woden-lithi's artists shows the sea giant, but he is named Y-M-R, hence Ymir. He is shown beside his ship (Figure 13-2), which is carried along the waves by a huge sea horse. The inscription reads Y-M-R N-GH-W (*Ymira nokwi*), readily translated as "The ship of Ymir." The giant may have been feared by Woden-lithi's mariners, so his defeat by Thunor would be cause for veneration of the Thunderer.

According to Snorri's *Edda*, the world will end with Ragnarök, the Twilight of the Gods, when the monsters of Jotunheim finally overcome the Aesir and Vanir. During the last battle Thor (Thunor of our Ontario text) manages to hold at bay the giant serpent that encircles the world and is called Midgardsormen (Worm of Middle Earth); at length his hammer Mjolnir avails no more, and Thunor and the other gods succumb. Parts of this scenario are depicted in various places on Woden-lithi's site.

A little west of a point 30 feet south of the main sun figure there can be found a number of serpents, with inscriptions scattered among them. The inscriptions (Figure 13-4) include M-O-L-N (*Mjolnir* of Old Norse), the hammer of Thunor; R-M (*orm*, "serpent" in Old Norse); M-D-N-M, apparently to be understood as *Midn[gardsorm] nama* ("Worm of Mid-Earth is its name"), *nama* being a south Germanic form, replacing *nefni* of Old Norse. Another serpent is labeled S-W, presumably *svika*, "twisting." The collection is identified (Figure 13-3) as R-G-N D-M (*Regin Domr*, Doom of the Gods). Another picture of the Worm of Mid-Earth appears in the engraving of Thunor given in an earlier chapter. The word A-K-W, Old Norse *akava*, is written beside yet another serpent: it means "fierce."

The earth is now given over to flame, and the Aesir gods under the leadership of Woden form in procession to ascend the rainbow (in Norse lore called Bridge-of-the-Gods) to enter Valhalla, there to await their own doom. This last scene is the subject of a petroglyph engraved some five feet southwest of the main sun-god

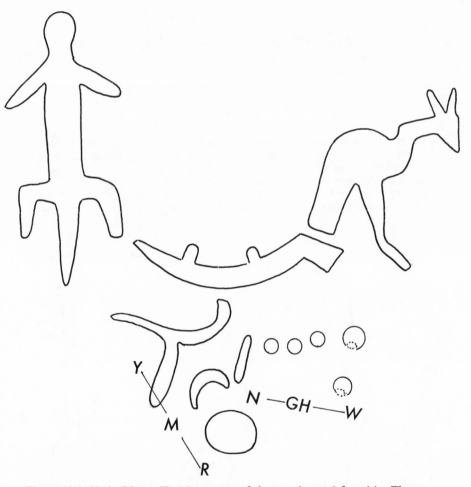

Figure 13-2. Ymir (Norse *Himir*) was one of the sea giants, defeated by Thunor with his hammer, Molnir. In this inscription Ymir is seen with his ship, N-GH-W (Norse *nokvi*), drawn by another monster, a sea horse. The inscription is located 15 feet south of the main sun-god figure at Peterborough.

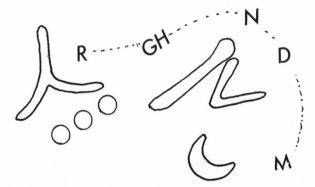

Figure 13-3. Regindom (Old Norse *Regindomr*, "Doom of the Gods"). This inscription, some 40 feet southwest of the main sun-god figure, relates to a series of labeled petroglyphs depicting serpents of Midgard (Middle Earth), who in conjunction with the monsters of Jotunheim (Under Earth) are about to overthrow the gods. Note the use of the second of the two letters that stand for *r*. Like Old Norse, which had two signs for *r*, Woden-lithi's tongue distinguishes two kinds of *r*-sound.

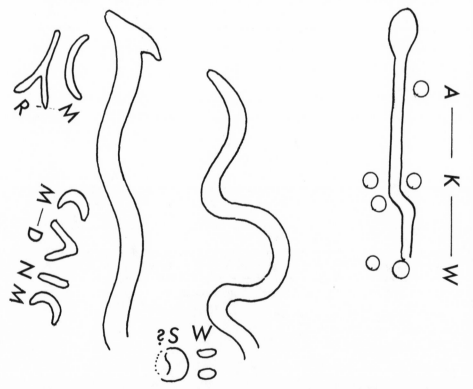

Figure 13-4. Same area as previous figure: serpent-dragons of Middle Earth. Left, R-M M-D N-M (*Orm Mid nama*, "Serpent of Mid[gard] by name." Middle, S(?)-W (*swi* [?], "venomous"); right A-K-W (*akwe*, "deadly, lethal").

figure (Figure 13-5). The petroglyph includes the Tifinag letters W-L-H-L, *Walhol,* which is also the Anglo-Saxon manner of pronouncing Valhalla. Inconsequent as it seems, perhaps because of the random manner in which the various pieces of Nordic mythology have been ground into the rock platform, a Yule-man seems to be taking part in the proceedings, wearing the disguise of the equinoctial hare, while he wrestles another clown dressed as a bear.

These ancient Nordic myths were to some extent acquired or inherited by the Algonquian and Sioux tribes who were the neighbors of the colonists. Pictographs and petroglyphs of dragons and other monsters found along the banks of the St. Lawrence present features remarkably like the monsters of Norse tradition.

Even more surprising is the persistence of these stories into quite modern times among the Takhelne of British Columbia, who speak a language derived in part from Celtic. In modern times, not more than one or two centuries ago at most, painted inscriptions, lettered in ogam script, were created by artists who not only recalled the form of the monsters, but also retained the ability to write the names of the supernatural beings in legible ogam script. An example of such work, depicting Loki and the dragon of Middle Earth, is shown in Figure 13-6. It serves as a visible reminder of how long a folk memory can persist if the demands of tribal tradition so require.

Figure 13-5. Ascent of the gods to Walhol (W-L-H-L). As Ragnarök (Twilight of the Gods) begins with the defeat of the Aesir by the monsters of Midgard (Middle Earth), Woden leads a procession across the rainbow (the bridge of the gods) to Valhalla. Whether the Yule-man (lower left) is part of the procession or merely accidentally in juxtaposition is uncertain. This part of the inscription lies 5 feet southwest of the main sun god figure. *Walhol* is the Anglo-Saxon form of the name Valhalla; it seems to be the form used by Woden-Lithi.

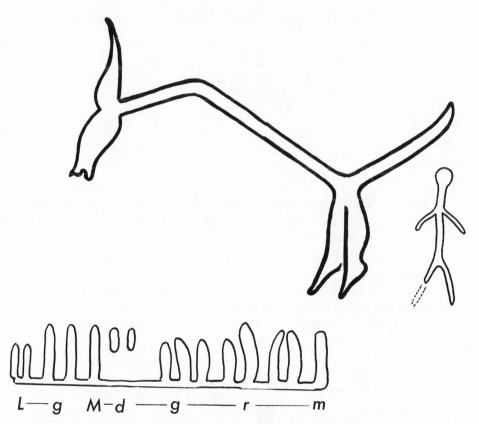

L —— g   M–d —— g —— r —— m

Figure 13-6. The American Indians have a long memory for ancient lore. This painted inscription, discovered by John Corner at his Site 48 in British Columbia, was probably executed barely two centuries ago. Its ogam text may be read as *Logi Midgar* [ds]-*orm*, "Loki and the Dragon of Middle Earth."

14

BUSINESS TRANSACTIONS
IN THE BRONZE AGE

Most of us, consciously or unconsciously, tend to interpret the past in terms of the present. Since we ourselves use trading tokens and coins, we assume that our remote ancestors may have done the same. But when did this custom begin? When was simple barter replaced by more sophisticated business dealings, involving standards of exchange comparable to coinage? In the 1950's I became interested in this question, and published my findings in two papers. The conclusions I reached are relevant to this chapter. The inquiry was prompted by events in Britain that resulted from World War II.

At that time the people of Britain faced a severe food shortage caused by the blockade of ships bringing farm products from overseas. To help overcome the crisis, every possible strip of land, no matter how narrow, was plowed and planted. Along the ancient highways, many of them going back to Roman or even Celtic times, the bordering verges of grass were put to the plow and then planted. But many an ancient foot-traveler had once wandered along these routes, occasionally dropping coins by mischance, or in other cases deliberately concealing pots of coins if danger threatened. Many a burial had remained intact when the owner had met with ill fate, or perhaps could no longer return, or failed to locate his treasure. Tens of thousands of ancient coins, Roman, Saxon, and medieval, were discovered by the plowmen. As a result the market value of ancient coins dropped with a crash, and it became possible for many people of quite modest means to assemble valuable and instructive collections of these intriguing relics of our ancestors.

Since the Anglo-Saxon silver pennies are the oldest inscribed artifacts we possess from the ill-documented period that followed the withdrawal of the Romans from Britain in the fifth century after Christ, I began to research the Old English manuscripts in an effort to discover what role these coins played in our ancestors' daily lives; later, as stated above, I summarized my findings in two papers published in 1954 and 1955. What at first puzzled me greatly was that nearly all the references to monetary transactions that occur in the Saxon literature are to *shillings, pounds,* and *marks*—yet the only coins that are found in the soil are *pennies* and pieces of lesser value, such as *feorthungs* (farthings, that is, quarters of a penny, cut with shears for change) and some irregular coins called *stykas,* issued in the first years of the Saxon occupation.

Now, a typical Saxon entry relating to money is represented by this passage, which I translate from the seventeenth-century laws of King Ine of Wessex: "If a man owns a hide of land, his *wer* [that is, property value] is to be reckoned at 120 shillings, half a hide 80 shillings, and if he owns no land 60 shillings." Apparently taxes were apportioned according to one's *wer.* Again, King Aethelberht, who died in the year 616, decreed that if a man had one ear smitten off in combat, the aggressor must pay him six shillings amends. There is a whole table of possible injuries and the appropriate compensation payable in each case—injury to the mouth, 12 shillings; loss of an eye, 50 shillings; the four front teeth, 6 shillings each; an eyetooth, 4 shillings; the first premolar, 3 shillings; other teeth a shilling each—and so on.

But what were these "shillings"? Certainly not the silver coins of that name that were first struck in England in the Middle Ages. It turns out that in Saxon times all these monetary terms were merely units of account. A shilling in nearly every case actually means a *sheep.* The true equations of account were as follows:

6 sheep equal 1 ox
8 oxen equal 1 man

30 silver pence equal 1 ox	48 shillings weigh one pound
5 silver pence equal 1 sheep	1 sheep equals 1 shilling
240 silver pence equal 1 man	1 man equals 1 pound of silver

Almost all debts were extinguished, not by coin of the realm (which was scarce) but by barter payments of sheep and oxen. The system remained almost intact until inflation set in, caused by labor scarcity during the Black Death (1349). Hence we may hazard the guess that the Saxon system was an ancient one, and that it had been introduced from Denmark and northern Germany, the homelands of the Angles, Jutes, and Saxons who invaded England after Roman rule ended.

According to the ancient historians of Greece and Rome, the oldest city in Europe is Cadiz (*Gades* of the ancients), founded by Phoenician traders in the twelfth century B.C. The Phoenician script rapidly spread through southern and western Spain and Portugal, soon assuming a characteristic *Iberian* form in which certain letters were written somewhat differently from their original form as developed in Phoenicia (Lebanon), where the parent cities of the Phoenicians, Tyre and Sidon, are located. Later, as the Phoenician colony of Carthage, in Tunisia, became independent, other varieties of Phoenician script arose and spread through the Iberian peninsula. In addition, mysterious scripts of apparently native Iberian origin occur in Spain and Portugal in archaeological contexts that certainly long antedate the Romans and may well antedate those of the Phoenician traders of Cadiz.

At the time when Cadiz was founded the Nordic peoples were settled in lands that we now call Germany and Scandinavia. Their cousins the Celts occupied much of Gaul and parts of Britain, and were beginning to penetrate into Spain. Much of the Iberian peninsula was peopled by tribes who probably spoke Basque, and the Basque philologist Imanol Agiŕe is of the opinion that Basque-speaking tribes were also to be found in Britain and Ireland as well as parts of Gaul.

Archaeological excavation discloses that these northern peoples were still in the Stone Age as late as 1800 B.C., and their emergence into the Bronze Age during the century that followed was occasioned by trade contact with Mediterranean peoples, from whom they obtained bronze swords and elaborate knives and other sophisticated manufactures. Apparently only the wealthiest members of Nordic society could afford these imported luxuries, for we find carefully chipped flint imitations of the bronze knives, apparently the property of commoners who could not afford to purchase the bronze originals. According to the ancient historians the Phoenicians traded with these northern peoples, taking such valuable wares as purple cloth for their chiefs, and the bronze weapons I have mentioned, and receiving in return such materials as tin from Cornwall and amber from the Baltic lands. A so-called amber route has been traced, leading from Denmark southward along the Danube to the Rumanian ports of the Black Sea. But was this the only door by which the Nordic peoples could face the trading world of the Mediterranean? It seems unlikely, for the Bronze Age rock carvings of Scandinavia depict fleets of ships similar to those of the Mediterranean peoples (especially the Libyans of North Africa), and such vessels could certainly cross the open sea.

An actual example of one of these vessels (though excavated from a site thought to date to about the fifth century B.C.) is known, and I had the privilege of examining it in Copenhagen in 1953. About 13 meters long, it is constructed in a manner very similar to that of the Polynesian oceangoing craft: that is to say, of adzed wooden planks held together, not by nails or dowels, but *sewn* together by cordage. With similar vessels, called *waka,* the ancient Polynesians could cross open spans of the Pacific of 3,000 miles, such as the gap between Tahiti and New Zealand. We know from carefully kept traditional Polynesian sources that the 3,000-mile journey was covered at a rate of 100 miles a day, so that a voyage to New Zealand lasted only a month; vegetable tubers were stored in the lower part of the hull, fish were caught each day, and rain supplemented the drinking water carried in gourds. Carbon dating has shown that human settlement of New Zealand had been achieved at least by the tenth century A.D., as Maori tradition also affirms.

The Polynesian voyages had spanned the Pacific in the centuries before the occupation of the southernmost region, New Zealand, and this historical fact is accepted without question by archaeologists. It has therefore always seemed strange to me, brought up in Polynesia as I was, that European and American archaeologists seem to have so much difficulty in conceiving that the people who built the Bronze Age ships of Europe could not also have made similar transoceanic voyages. However, leaving aside for the moment the question of transoceanic sailing, it is surely not to be doubted that the Scandinavian skippers of the Bronze Age must certainly have made voyages along the coasts of the Baltic and the North Sea. It is inconceivable that any people who inhabited a sea-girt land would build ships if it were not their avocation or profession to sail wheresoever their fancy and sea skills sufficed to prompt adventure or trading voyage.

Inevitably the Scandinavians must have discovered that Phoenician ships and traders were working the western approaches to Europe. Inevitably their interest would turn upon the valuable trade goods of Phoenicia, available to them either by peaceable trading of the Baltic amber that the Semitic visitors so much craved, or by piratical attack if circumstances might make such a course seem profitable. Homer and Hesiod, both of whom wrote of the Greek mariners of the Bronze Age, tell us that farmers turned pirate during the summer and returned to reap their crops in the fall, bringing ill-gotten treasure and Phoenician slave women as booty from the summer's expeditions. I think it may be taken as given that the ancient Norsemen would do much the same.

If, then, the Bronze Age Norsemen encountered Phoenician or Iberian traders, either as visitors to their own lands, or as people to whose shores they themselves paid visits, would they not acquire from them a knowledge of writing skills? It seems they did indeed, as the following implies.

One of the best known of the Danish archaeological sites is that located at Mullerup Mose, in the western part of the island of Zealand. The older name of the site was Maglemose, and under the latter name there has been designated a Stone Age culture whose remains are found there. The site, like many others of the Stone Age, spans a long period of time, in this case thought to range from about 7000 B.C. down to 1500 B.C. Its later elements, if the dating is correct, would therefore overlap with the onset of the Bronze Age, in the shape of the first trading visitors from Phoenician Iberia, or the return of Norse ships from visits to Iberia.

Among the curious artifacts attributed to the Maglemose people are a series of engraved bones (Figure 14-1), the purpose of which would be hard to determine were it not for the fact, hitherto overlooked, that small inscriptions in the Iberic alphabet can be found on some of them.

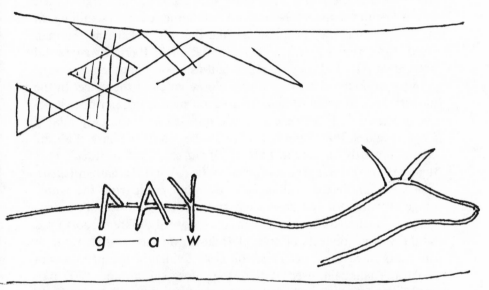

Figure 14-1. Some of the engraved bone artifacts found near Mullerup Mose, Denmark, and attributed to Neolithic industry, are in fact of much later date. This example recorded by P. Reinecke, is lettered in Iberian-Phoenician script and dates from between 1500 and 1200 B.C. It is a trader's receipt for the purchase of cloth by payment of one cow's value of barter goods. The word *wag*, to be read from right to left in the Semitic manner, is one of the ancient Indo-European roots, meaning a heifer or cow. It survives in Iberia today as *vaca*, and related forms occur in all the Romance languages.

We find engravings of oxen (cows or heifers) and, beside them, or drawn separately, meshwork patterns that can be recognized as the common European symbol for cloth or weaving, often found engraved on loom weights, for example. On one engraving of a cow we find the Iberic letters that spell (reading from right to left in the Semitic manner) W-'A-G. The middle letter, resembling an A, is the letter 'alif, pronounced like the initial *A* in the German word *Apfel:* that is, with a slight glottal click. Iberian writers did not use vowels, and they regarded 'alif as a consonant. So the word is to be pronounced as *wag,* with a glottal catch in the voice. In the modern Scandinavian tongues there is no such word, nor does it occur in the related Teutonic tongues, nor in the less closely related Celtic tongues. But in the Latin family the root is the base of all the common words for cow in Latin itself (*vacca*), Spanish (*vaca*), Portuguese (*vaca*), French (*vache*), Italian (*vaca*) and Rumanian (*vacǎ*). The Swiss philologist Julius Pokorny, after comparing the whole range of words for cow in ancient and modern Indo-European languages, concluded that there were once several different roots used by the various dialects of ancient Indo-Europeans, and that one of the roots must have been *uak* or *wak.* Evidently the people who spoke the language used at the Maglemose site around 1500 B.C. used that particular root, and pronounced the terminal guttural as a *g* rather than a *k.* This does not necessarily mean that the Maglemose people were not Nordic, or that they were displaced members of the Latin group. It probably merely means that the word *wag* was widely recognized by the various trading peoples of Bronze Age Europe as being a term for cow. And why should a cow be depicted, and labeled in writing, on a bone, beside a depiction of fabric?

The answer is not far to seek. Beside one of the engravings of the symbol for cloth we find the Iberic letters that spell Q-D (Figure 14-2), which is the Phoenician manner of writing KH-D, the vowel as usual left unexpressed. This word again matches an Indo-European root identified by Pokorny: *kwei-,* with a terminal -*d* as the sign of the past participle. It answers to the modern English word *quit* and the Old Norse *kveitr,* as well as many other modern and ancient European forms of the root, all conveying the sense of "quittance" or "paid." In fact, these bones are evidently receipts issued by some trader to persons who have purchased from him cloth

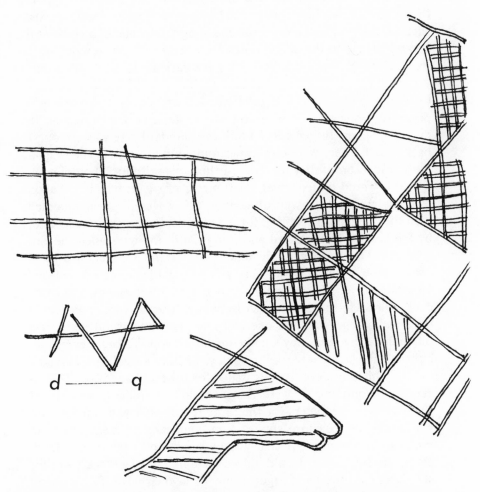

Figure 14-2. Another Bronze Age receipt from the Danish Maglemose (Mullerup Mose) region, mistaken for Neolithic decorative work. It is engraved on bone, records the purchase of one cow's-worth of cloth, and is inscribed Q-D, representing the ancient Indo-European word meaning quittance or receipt for a payment made.

to the value of 6 shillings: that is to say, one cow. And to support this inference we have in the Old Norse language special words, such as *kugildi* and *kyrlag,* both meaning "the value of a cow" and corresponding to the Saxon unit of 6 sheep or 30 pence, equaling 1 ox (see above). The equation may have varied a little; for example, we know that in one English summer, sheep had become so plentiful that the exchange rate (*angilde*) fell drastically and became 3 pence to 1 sheep, so that a cow would then only be rated at 18 pieces of silver. In general, I think the standard rate was the one I have stated. There were no pennies minted in the days of the Maglemose trader, but if they had been, I think his price for a bolt of woven cloth would be reckoned as 30 pieces of silver, which in Saxon terms is yet another way of saying "the wages of an able-bodied man for one month's work," for a Saxon earned a penny a day and, by the laws of King Alfred and King Guthrum, who ruled the English and Danes, "An Englishman and a Dane are reckoned as of equal value." (Their wives were not so regarded. The present-day advocates of equal rights for women may trace their complaints back at least to the era we are discussing, when a woman was reckoned as having a value of one half-man, and was accordingly paid one half-penny for a day's labor in the harvest. To buy her bolt of cloth, then, she must work for 60 days or have a wealthy husband.)

And why were receipts issued for the purchase of goods? Receipts or "quittances" were the invention of traders, who issued them to their customers for the same reason that your modern supermarket or drugstore staples a mechanically printed receipt to your purchase—to prove that you have not stolen the goods. Traders in ancient Europe would indeed have had to keep a wary eye for shoplifters, as dozens of eager farmers and their wives fingered and examined the wares. After a purchase was made, the customer would be given a formal receipt, already engraved in advance at the stipulated value. Complaints against shoplifters could then more easily be handled by the local chieftain, who would know that no more visits from traders could be expected unless he saw to it that due restitution was made. With such homely materials as these pieces of engraved bone, the life of our remote ancestors acquires a new dimension, one much more familiar to us than the notion that they were savage barbarians.

15
WHAT THE GRAVE GOODS
TELL US

An important part in the recognition of the language and origins of ancient peoples consists in studying their grave goods closely in search of inscriptions. Small but telltale comments or notations often occur on objects that look unimportant but that formed some part of household or artisan's equipment. For example, loom weights may carry a notation indicating whether they belong to the warp of a standing loom or to the pairs of threads that form part of a so-called cardloom. Archaeologists are prone to overlook these, supposing them to be some decorative marking of no significance. Thus, Basque token coins of the second century B.C., issued in imitation of Aquitanian silver coins of the Celts and carrying an ogam statement in the Basque language have been erroneously identified as "buttons" or "necklace beads," and classified as Aurignacian artifacts of 20,000 B.C. In America stone loom weights, labeled in ogam with the Celtic word meaning "warp," have been identified as Amerindian "gorgets." Pottery impress stamps, labeled to that effect in Iberic script, have been mistaken for decorated combs. Cases could be multiplied of similar mistakes. The errors arise from the fact that archaeologists often do not realize what important light epigraphers can throw on their finds, and that what may be mistaken for mere decoration is often an ancient form of script, which can identify the people who once owned and used the artifacts.

The occurrence of burials with associated inscribed relics was first reported for North America in 1838, when a tumulus at Grave Creek, Moundsville, West Virginia, was excavated and yielded an inscribed stone tablet, obviously written in some alphabet related to the Phoenician or Carthaginian. When a Danish authority on scripts, Dr. Rafn at Copenhagen University, was sent a copy of the writing on the stone, he promptly identified it as being in one of the Iberian scripts. As Grave Creek is 300 miles from the sea, the implication seemed to be that an Iberian settlement had once occurred in North America—a notion that later archaeologists rejected. Hence the Grave Creek grave goods and the included tablet were either forgotten or attributed to the treacherous invention of forgers.

In more recent times more artifacts have been found with inscriptions in Iberic (as well as other ancient European scripts) and have been recorded and published, but only as "decorated" artifacts. Since archaeologists did not expect to find inscribed artifacts, they were unaware of what might constitute an inscribed artifact. Dr. William P. Grigsby of east Tennessee, who has assembled one of the largest collections of excavated artifacts of eastern North America, began, after reading my *America B.C.,* to recognize on some of his specimens markings that appeared to match both Iberian letters and ogam script; he wrote to draw my attention to his specimens and then allowed me to research them.

When the attention of archaeologists was drawn to the presence of ogam inscriptions on the artifacts as also on some of the megalithic chambers, their response was often disbelief, as I have said. Their scepticism is based on the mistaken notion, long held, "that ogam was invented no earlier than the fourth century A.D., for use in Ireland." The best answer to criticisms of the kind cited lies in numismatics, for dates of coins can be established with considerable accuracy.

Illustrated in Figure 15-1 are two Celtic silver coins of the second century B.C. They are imitations of the coinage of a Greek trading center in Spain named Emporiom. The lower example, which dates from before 133 B.C., is lettered in Iberian script, and reads *nomse,* the Celtiberian version of the original Greek word for a coin, *nomisma.* The upper example is drawn from a specimen, now in the British Museum, of a silver coin of the Gauls of Aquitania. It has been dated (Allen, *Celtic Coins,* British Museum, 1978) to the second century before Christ. The ogam inscription is in

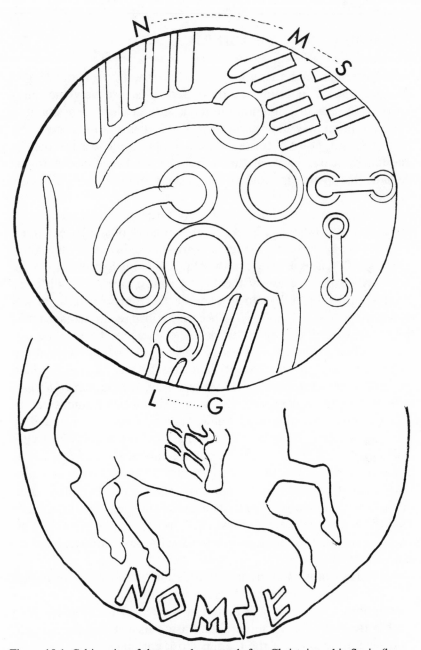

Figure 15-1. Celtic coins of the second century before Christ, issued in Spain (lower example) and in Aquitania (upper example). Both are imitations of the silver coinage of the Iberian Greek city of Emporion, and both carry the word *nomse* (coinage), the upper example written in ogam consaine, the lower in Iberian letters. Examples such as these disprove the current belief that ogam was a British invention dating from the end of the Roman era.

ogam consaine and therefore omits the vowels. It reads N-M-S (*nomse,* coin), and below are the letters L-G, probably the mint-mark of the city of Lugdunum in Aquitania. A clear photograph of the inscription may be seen on page 35 of Allen's *Celtic Coins.*

This disposes of the claim I cited that "ogam was invented in the fourth century A.D. at the earliest." I shall now deal with the remark that ogam "is peculiar to the Celts and in particular to the Irish."

The bone disk with an engraved design and ogam inscription, shown in Figure 15-2, is one of a number of similar examples found at the palaeolithic site at Laugerie-Basse, in the Basque country of the Pyrenees adjacent to the old Celtic kingdom of Aquitania, from which the previously mentioned coin derives. This disk has been identified by archaeologists as "a bead from a necklace, or less probably, a button," and it has been described as an artifact made by the cave-dwelling Paleolithic people of Laugerie-Basse.

These statements cannot be correct. The ogam consaine inscription reads in the Basque language S-H-T (*šehe-te*), which means "to serve as money." More precisely, the standard *Diccionario* of Azukue explains that the word refers to what numismatists call a billon coin of very small value; "billon" means a debased alloy of silver. Clearly the bone disk is a Basque imitation of the Celtic coinage of Aquitania and can be dated to about the same period as the piece it simulates: the second century B.C. Like many other inscriptions of ancient Europe—and America—it has nothing to do with Ireland, nor does it express a Celtic tongue. It is improbable that the engravers of any of these coins were "familiar with the Latin language," nor should such a familiarity have any relevance to the subject.

Many other Celtiberian and Gaulish numismatic examples of ogam consaine can be cited. However, I need now to refer to the inscriptions found in North America, written in Iberic script (like that of the Grave Creek mound) and using Basque or other Iberian language. In the case of the Iberian script cut on stones in Pennsylvania, and reported by me as Basque in 1974, the *Basque Encyclopedia* now includes these inscriptions as the earliest recognized Basque writing, but in contrast the American archaeologists claim that they are marks made by roots of trees or by plowshares. When

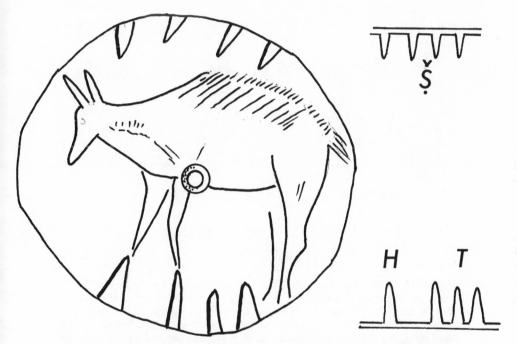

Figure 15-2. Token coinage made from bone, circulating in the Basque provinces adjacent to the Celtic kingdom of Aquitania in the second century before Christ. The ogam inscription reads, in Basque language, "To serve as money." This token and similar bone tokens from the same region are presently classified by archaeologists as "either beads or, less probably, buttons, made by the palaeolithic people of Laugerie-Basse, and datable to about 20,000 B.C. On such mistaken premises the occurrence of genuine ogam inscriptions at numerous sites in America and in Europe of pre-Roman times, has been ignored.

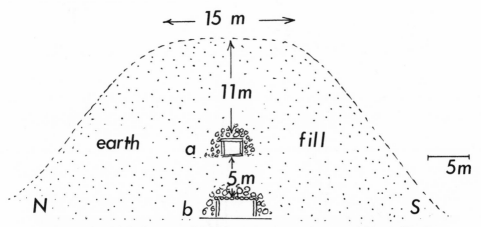

Figure 15-3. Main features of the Grave Creek tumulus, near Moundsville, West Virginia. The lower chamber, with a long axis directed north and south, length 12 feet, height 7 feet, contained remains of two skeletons. The upper chamber, of the same proportions, but directed east and west, contained a single burial, accompanied by grave goods that included the tablet of stone shown in the previous illustration. Rafn of Copenhagen University recognized the script as being Iberic, and the exact form of the letters was checked by Henry R. Schoolcraft, who visited the site and made a mold of the stone tablet, from which he later published the illustration. Despite these early evidences of Iberian penetration into North America, archaeologists still have difficulty in accepting the reality of the Iberian and other Old World inscriptions being found today with other grave goods on ancient cemetery sites, in various parts of North America.

Dr. Grigsby first discovered the Iberian script on some of his artifacts, the signs he found were precisely the same set of letters that
make up the Iberic alphabet, and which had earlier been found on
the grave markers and boundary stones of Pennsylvania. Asked if
these markings are caused by miniature plows, archaeologists have
thus far maintained a stony silence.

There are also quite independent and unrelated reasons for
thinking that ancient European voyagers came to America. They
concern the mining of metals.

For the past twenty years leading mining engineers and university metallurgists have been seeking from archaeologists an explanation of a most baffling mystery in the history of mining
technology. So far no answer has been found.

Around the northern shore of Lake Superior, and on the adjacent Ile Royale, there are approximately 5,000 ancient copper
mine workings. In 1953 and 1956 Professor Roy Drier led two
Michigan Mining and Technology expeditions to the sites. Charcoal
found at the bases of the ancient mining pits yielded radiocarbon
dates indicating that the mines had been operated between 2000 B.C.
and 1000 B.C. These dates correspond nearly to the start and the
end of the Bronze Age in northern Europe. The most conservative
estimates by mining engineers show that at least 500 million pounds
of metallic copper were removed over that time span, and there is
no evidence as to what became of it.

Archaeologists have maintained that there was no Bronze
Age in Northern America and that no contacts with the outside
world occurred. On the other hand, the mineralogists find themselves obliged to take a different view: it is impossible, they argue,
for so large a quantity of metal to have vanished through wear and
tear. And since no large numbers of copper artifacts have been recovered from American archaeological sites, they conclude that the
missing metal may have been shipped overseas. Such an opinion, as
is obvious, now becomes entirely reasonable, for the inscriptions of
Woden-lithi declare that copper ingots were his primary target in
coming to Canada. Previous shippers must have passed the information to the Norse king, since otherwise he could not have known
that copper was available and that a suitable trade commodity in
exchange would be woven fabrics and cordage.

Thus the sum total of evidence from burial sites, from the chance discovery of burial marker stones and boundary stones, from the other sources mentioned in this book, all adds up to a consistent and simple explanation of all the baffling facts; it is simply this—European colonists and traders have been visiting or settling in the Americas for thousands of years, have introduced their scripts and artifacts and skills, and have exported abroad American products such as copper.

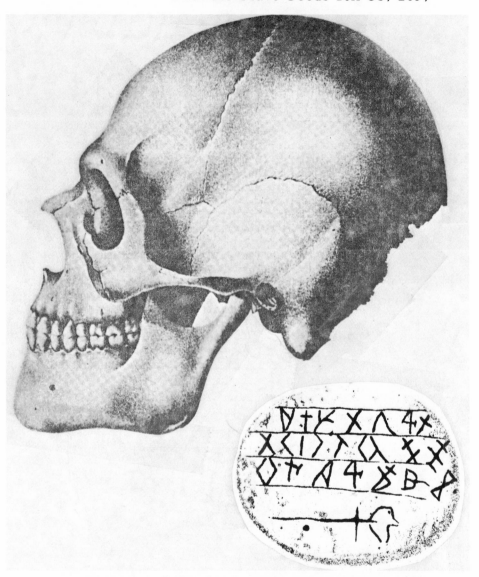

Figure 15-4. Skull from the upper chamber and associated inscribed tablet in Iberian script, from the Grave Creek tumulus, West Virginia. Iberian scholars recognize the writing as Iberian. Two more tablets of the same type have since been discovered in regions adjacent to Grave Creek, where numerous smaller tumuli also occur. There appears to be no sound reason for supposing that the mounds are something peculiarly American, or that the inscribed tablets are forgeries. The evidence is strongly in favor of an Iberian presence in Ancient America.

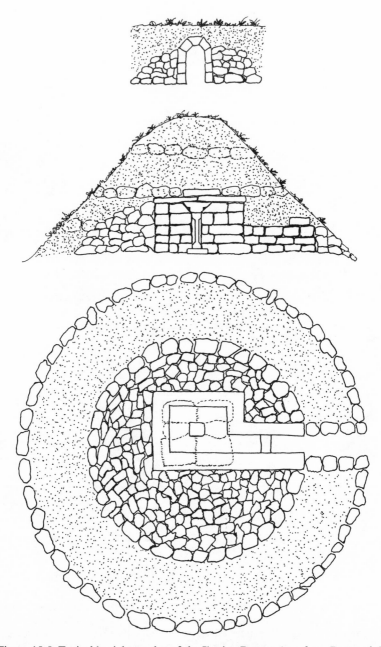

Figure 15-5. Typical burial tumulus of the Iberian Bronze Age, from Portugal. The mound is 60 feet high, matching that of the Grave Creek mound in West Virginia. But the burial chamber is constructed of fitted stones, whereas the North America example used timber covered by loose stone fill. With rotting of the wood, the chamber in the Grave Creek mound collapsed, whereas the Portuguese example did not.

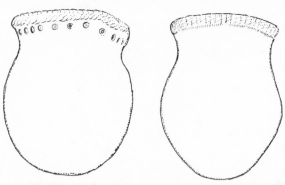

Figure 15-6. Bell-shaped unglazed funerary urns were introduced into the Iberian Peninsula toward the close of the European Bronze Age, around 800 B.C. Archaeologists of Spain, Portugal and France believe that these vessels were brought to Spain by Celts of the Urnfield culture in France. They usually have an incised geometric pattern, especially around the rim. Of the pair of urns shown above, the one on the left was excavated from a pre-Iroquois site at Owasco, New York, The one on the right is from Marles, near Barcelona. Pottery of this type appears abruptly in New England sites at about the same time as its introduction into Spain. As pottery is lacking from sites of earlier date in the northeastern states, its sudden appearances, replacing carved soapstone bowls, points to an influx of people with a new culture, and the style of the vessels points to a probable origin in Iberia.

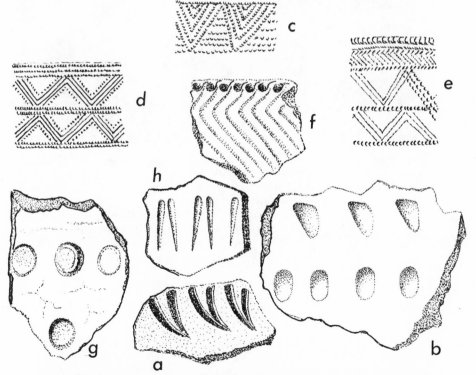

Figure 15-7. Incised patterns from bell-shaped and similar pottery urns: c, d, from Las Cogotas, Portugal, late Bronze Age; e, from New York State; a, b, f, g, h, all from Amoskeag, New Hampshire (collection of James Whittall). At the early Woodland site investigated by the Archaeological Society of Tennessee at Snapp's Bridge, Tennessee, artifacts engraved in Iberian and ogam script were discovered, incuding a pottery stamp of the kind used to produce the incised patterns.

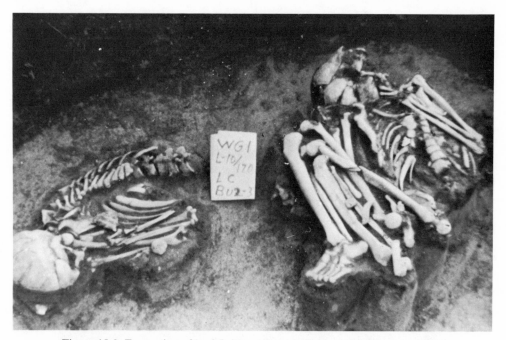

Figure 15-8. Excavation of burial sites at Snapp's Bridge, east Tennessee, by members of the Tennessee Archaeological Society brought to light flexed interments of individuals accompanied by artifacts, some of which proved to carry finely engraved inscriptions. The burials and the nature of the associated artifacts presented many similarities to early Bronze Age burials in Portugal and Spain, where round-skulled (brachycephalic) people with a variable degree of jaw projection (mesognathous jaws) occur, yielding skull characters very much like those of southeastern Amerindians. *Photo William P. Grigsby.*

Figure 15-9. Supposed bone comb, found in one of the Snapp's Bridge burials by members of the Archaeological Society of Tennessee. The "decoration," however, proves to be an inscription in Celtiberian, indicating that the artifact is in reality a stamp for imprinting patterns on unfired pottery. *Photo Peter J. Garfall.*

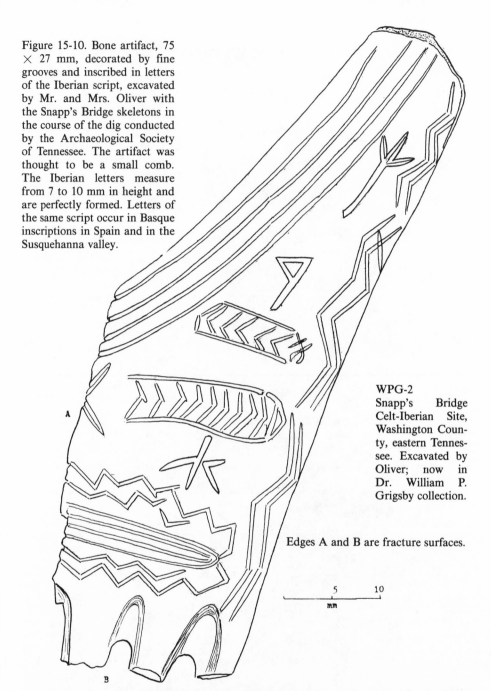

Figure 15-10. Bone artifact, 75 × 27 mm, decorated by fine grooves and inscribed in letters of the Iberian script, excavated by Mr. and Mrs. Oliver with the Snapp's Bridge skeletons in the course of the dig conducted by the Archaeological Society of Tennessee. The artifact was thought to be a small comb. The Iberian letters measure from 7 to 10 mm in height and are perfectly formed. Letters of the same script occur in Basque inscriptions in Spain and in the Susquehanna valley.

A

WPG-2
Snapp's Bridge Celt-Iberian Site, Washington County, eastern Tennessee. Excavated by Oliver; now in Dr. William P. Grigsby collection.

Edges A and B are fracture surfaces.

5   10
mm

B

Matching letters, when found engraved on rocks, have been considered as "marks made by plowshares." Basque readings, published by the author, have been confirmed by Agire, the Basque lexicographer. For the decipherment of the inscription on this artifact, see Figure 15-11.

T

R

fracture

C

Figure 15-11. The letters conform to Greek early styles of the 8th to 5th centuries B.C., and are to be read in boustrophedon. Rectified to modern order we have:

C-L C-R-T (*Clo criata*, Imprint-stamp for pottery)

Thus the artifact is a potter's tool for imprint-the surface relief on wet unfired pottery. The existence of such stamps was inferred from the neat, uniform aspect of the surface patterns on the "Early Woodland" pottery found in the graves.

L— C

All epigraphers are indebted to the alertness of Dr. William P. Grigsby, who first noticed the unexplained letters on the artifacts exhumed by the Archaeological Society of Tennessee, purchased the collections, and then made them available for epigraphic research.

A	▽, ▷, A	I,Y	Ͷ, Ͷ, I	R	◁, Ρ, ϙ, ◊, φ
B,P	Γ, Γ, P, P, ⊗	L	Λ, 1, Λ, Λ	S,Š	Ϟ, Ϡ, ᛜ
C,K,G	⟨, ⟨, Ϗ, ⟨	M	ᚶ, ᛗ	T	Ψ, Ψ
D	✕, Ð	N	Ͷ, Ͷ	U,V,W	↑
E	▷, ℰ, ‖, Ͱ	O	Ͱ, ℙ, ⅅ, ◊	Z	Ɀ

Figure 15-12. The Iberian alphabet. The French numismatist A. Heiss, in his *Monnaies antiques de l'Espagne*, Paris (1870), solved the sound values of the letters used by the Celtiberians by comparing the Latin names of Spanish cities with coin lettering.

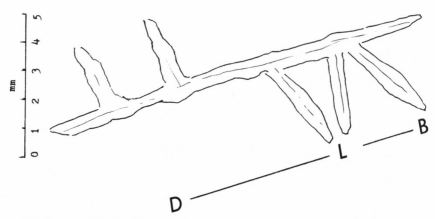

Figure 15-13. Ogam inscription on loom weight, face A, enlarged. Celtiberian, D-L-B (Gaelic *dealb*, "warp").

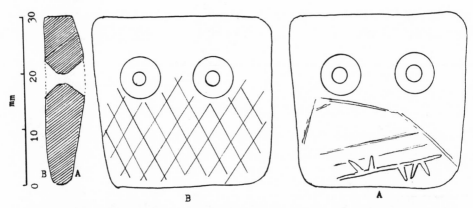

Both faces, and section, of warp-weight, part of grave goods found with flexed skeletons, Snapp's Bridge site, east Tennessee, excavated by the Archaeological Society of Tennessee; Grigsby Collection.

Loom weight (*pesa de telar*) from Castillo de Olarizu, Spain (J. M. Barandiaran, 1979, p. 178). Celtic Iron Age.

16

HOW STONE AGE LANGUAGE WAS PRESERVED IN BRONZE AGE PETROGLYPHS

It is now nearly twenty years since a Swiss scholar, Dr. Rudolph Engler, drew attention to the extraordinary similarity that exists between the rock carvings of ships engraved in Scandinavia during the Bronze Age and certain rock carvings found in North America. Dr. Engler's name and his thought-provoking book *Die Sonne als Symbol* (The Sun as a Symbol) are still little known in America, unfortunately. He expressed the opinion that an explanation for the facts would one day be supplied by epigraphic research. Certain easily recognizable symbols are found beside the Scandinavian ship engravings, and the identical symbols occur beside the American ones. When Engler wrote his book, however, none of the symbols had been deciphered, and consequently the writing—for such it appeared to be—remained unread and mysterious. We may speculate as to whether the Scandinavian rock engravings of ships may conceal a message unperceived by us because of the infantile aspect of the art itself.

One way to examine the matter is to let our mind's eye escape from the trammels of the age in which we happen to be born, and to take flight in fancy through time and space, to watch the artists at work (Figures 16-1 and 16-2).

Our first stop is to be on the Baltic seashore at Namforsen, in the Gulf of Bothnia, in northern Sweden. As we touch down, a Bronze Age artist has just engraved a representation of a ten-oared boat, with the crewmen represented as plain sticklike marks. He now takes up his gouge and hammers out a bent left arm on each of two facing crewmen. Next, to our surprise, he adds what seems an utterly irrelevant detail, a stylistic head of a horse suspended in midair (so it would seem) above the vessel's stern. Next we take flight southward to the island of Sjaelland, in Denmark, to watch another artist at work near Engelstrup. He has chosen to decorate a boulder. First he carves a stylized ship, a twenty-oared vessel. Again the crewmen are shown like vertical pegs. He now adds two more men, one at the bow and one suspended above the other rowers. Each of these two figures is now given a bent arm. Next (and this time we are prepared for it) he adds a horse in midair above the stern. Now we take flight across the Atlantic to visit one of King Wotan-lithi's artists. He, too, has cut a ship engraving, some 15 feet due east of the main sun figure. He has cut only 6 rowers. He now adds a larger stick figure at the bow, taking care to bend the forearm. Last, as we expect him to do, he adds a somewhat misshapen horse, suspended over the stern.

As we watch, he then walks across the site to a point that lies about 12 feet southwest of the central sun figure, where other engravers have begun to lay out the figures of a zodiac. He cuts a four-oared ship. Beside it he engraves a man in the bow and a very pregnant woman in the stern, and above them he engraves a large ring-shaped motif. Meanwhile, our Swedish and Danish artists have been busy. When we return to Engelstrup we find that the Dane has added a second ship to his boulder. Beside it he has placed two figures, a man and a woman, and between them he has engraved a very conspicuous ring-shaped object. As for the Swede, in his remote Bothnian fastness, when we arrive there we find he too has added a second ship, has carved a man and a pregnant woman beside it, and over their heads he has placed a ring-shaped design.

Now, to an epigrapher, a sequence such as I have just described—and the actual engravings do exist, at the places named— can mean only one thing: the artists in each case were following a

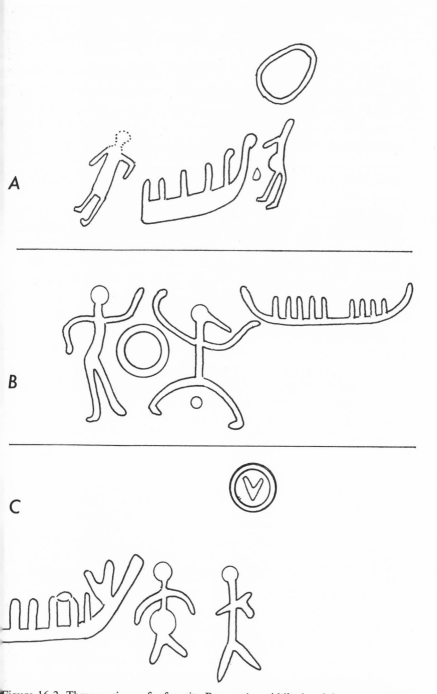

Figure 16-2. Three versions of a favorite Bronze Age riddle, involving a man, his pregnant wife, and a wedding ring. See text for explanation. A, version carved at the Peterborough site, Ontario. B, version carved at Engelstrup in Denmark. C, version carved at Namforsen, Sweden.

Figure 16-1. Three versions of a Bronze Age riddle using pictog
The upper example is at Peterborough, Ontario. The middle exam
gelstrup, Denmark, and the lower one from Sweden.

formalistic, well-defined system of writing. The scribes of ancient Egypt had similar procedures. Egyptian writing depends on the use of the rebus—a word that is easy to depict as a picture is used to indicate another word that sounds the same but that cannot be represented by a picture. Here is the principle, as the Egyptians developed it. Suppose you want to write the word *man* or *male.* That is easy, for you can make a little pictograph, a matchstick figure or a more elaborate one, depicting a man. The reader sees a man, and is expected to read "man," as indeed he will. But suppose you wanted to write, not *man,* but *brother.* That is much more difficult, for no matter how accurately you depict your own or someone else's brother, the average reader (who knows neither of the persons) will just say "man." How can you make him understand that the word intended is *brother?* The Egyptian discovery lies in the fact that in the Egyptian language the word *brother* is pronounced like *sen.* But in that language there is another, readily depictable, thing that was also called *sen*—namely, a ladle. So the solution is to draw a pictograph of a man, and then beside it place a pictograph of a ladle.

All that then is needed is to ensure that you teach your young people to read, and that in turn means teaching them to recognize in each word a *classifier* (or *determinant*) and a second element called the *phonoglyph* (sound-giver). In the word *brother* the man picture is the classifier, telling the reader that the word has something to do with male human beings, and the ladle picture is the phonoglyph, telling the reader that the male human has a name that sounds like *sen.*

When I lived in Copenhagen I became acquainted with Icelanders, whose language has preserved most of the features of Old Norse. They delight in word-play and also are noted for the high proportion of poets in their population. One whom I knew used to invent risqué punning games to tease some innocent party (usually me, since I spoke with a foreign accent, a rare thing for my Scandinavian friends, who felt that few foreigners cared to learn their language). He would first dream up some complicated pun in Danish and then make me say what appeared to be a harmless statement, the others present waiting breathless to see what would result. When I knew the words, he would then say "Faster, say it more quickly," whereupon the entire room would dissolve in laughter. To my innocent inquiry I would then be told that, by saying the words faster, I had made them run together to form a totally different and usually quite obscene statement: one of those Old Norse customs for whiling away the long winter nights along the Arctic Circle. In Polynesia I encountered similar customs, there called riddles and taken very seriously by some anthropologists whose knowledge of the language was too slight to enable them to realize the traps they were led into. I have seen, as a consequence, whole articles in the *Journal of the Polynesian Society* in which the unwary authors have reproduced scores of the most scurrilous material, thinly disguised as something different by dividing the words in different places. These so-called riddles were also a means of passing the long evenings. Also, tribal lore deemed to be too sacred for ordinary ears can be concealed in complex puns that the uninitiated does not fully comprehend.

With these experiences in mind, and knowing now as we do that the language spoken by the Bronze Age engravers of Scandinavia and Ontario is a Nordic language, we can test whether the inconsequential assemblages of horses in midair, men with bent arms, and rings gazed upon by male and female matchstick figures may be written puns, like ancient Egyptian hieroglyphs. The test, of course, is to utter aloud the names of the depicted objects in sequence.

Since the Danish example carries both of the statements on the same stone, one above the other, we will use that one.

In English we have: (reading each line from left to right):
English: People, arms bent, and a horse. A man and a woman at a ring gaze.
Norse: Menneskjor, olna kviesand'ok hrossr. Ok mann ok kvinna't hring da.
Homophone: Menne kjol-nakvi Suna dagi hrossa, ok man-nokvi natt hrinda.
English: Men to the keeled sun-ship at dawn give praise, and to the moon-ship at her night launching.

Thus, the seemingly childish pictures are readily seen to be not pictures, but hieroglyphs. They are, in my opinion, examples of Stone Age writing, poetic and religious, hallowed by centuries of use before the Bronze Age and carefully preserved intact as historic and religious expressions of piety from a former age.

By treating the messages of the Bronze Age as literal and childish, we have completely failed to interpret the true sense they impart. The rock-cut petroglyphs deserve the close attention of linguists, who may be expected to produce more perfect interpretations than those I can offer. I am not an expert on any one of the many languages I decipher, but I do tend to see the woods rather than the individual trees. I think linguists are prone to spend so much time splitting hairs over dictionary-authorized spellings and grammatical niceties that they often forget that ancient peoples had no dictionaries, no written standards of spelling, and that the grammar of each hamlet and village was likely to deviate from that of its neighbors.

17
WHO WERE THE SEA PEOPLES?

Before closing this account of Nordic exploration in the far northern seas we should pause to take some cognizance of events in the Mediterranean world at the onset of the twelfth century B.C. These were turbulent times in the southern lands, where violent attacks by a mysterious group of raiders referred to as the Sea Peoples laid in ruins the Aegean civilization and even threatened the very survival of the Egyptian monarchy. Egypt at this time was ruled by one of the most powerful of the Pharaohs, Ramesses III, who reigned from 1188 to 1165 B.C.

Whereas only the smoke-stained ruins now remain to speak mutely of the onslaught that suddenly struck down the peaceful trading empire of the Aegean peoples, as they fell victims to the raiders from the sea, in Egypt a stout and effective resistance was made against the pirates, adequate warning having no doubt reached the Nile Delta when the disasters occurred in the archipelago to the north of Egypt. As to what happened next, we are almost wholly dependent upon Egyptian records carved at Medinet Habu to memorialize the defeat by Ramesses III of the Libyans and Sea Peoples in 1194 and 1191 B.C., and a final attack in 1188 B.C. by yet one more wave of Sea Peoples, this time not from Libya but from the east. In the bas-reliefs that depict the naval battles (Figure 17-1), the defeated Sea Peoples are represented as having a European cast of face. Some of them are shown wearing hemispherical helmets that carry two recurved upward-directed horns. For other clothing they wear a kilt. Their weapons are swords and spears,

Detail, monument of Ramesses III at Medinet Habu, twelfth century B.C.

Figure 17-1. Various tribes of maritime nations attacked Egypt from the sea during the early decades of the twelfth century before Christ. The Egyptians called them by the collective name "Sea Peoples." To judge by the Egyptian sculptors' depictions at the monument of Ramesses III at Medinet Habu, some of the Sea Peoples appear to have been Nordic, as in the above detail. Ramesses defeated the invaders, who then sailed westward to land in Libya. In Libya the Tifinag alphabet survives in use to this day, but in Bronze Age times it was peculiar to the Nordic peoples. The facts suggest that Nordic invaders, rebuffed from Egypt, settled Libya and introduced the Tifinag alphabet at that time.

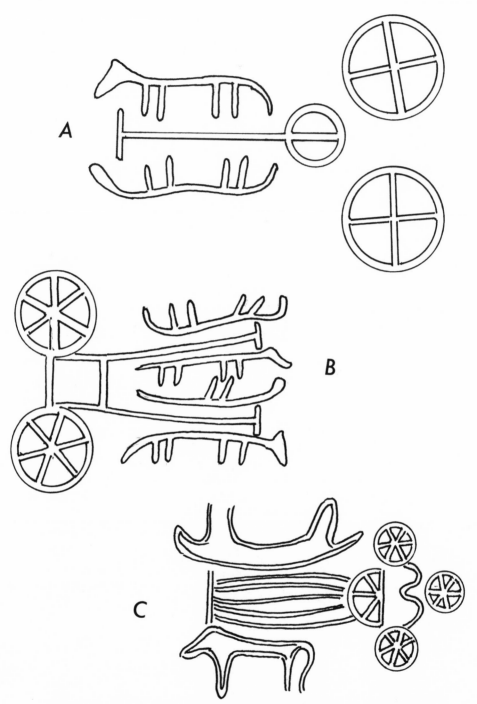

Figure 17-2. Apparent Bronze Age links between the Nordic world and North Africa. A, petroglyph at Kirchspiel Askum, Germany, showing the solar disk conveyed on a horse-drawn vehicle. B, petroglyph at Oued Zigra, Fezzan, and C, at Arli, Adrar des Iforas, in similar style, the latter apparently depicting the solar disk drawn on a two-horse vehicle.

whereas the Egyptian marines are armed with bows and arrows, and are shown able to attack the invaders with a fusillade before the Sea Peoples could come near enough to board the Egyptian vessels. According to Ramesses III, the defeated remnants of these invaders fled westward to Libya. Two centuries later the descendants of the invaders seized power in Egypt, reigning as the XXII or Libyan dynasty for a span of 200 years.

The suggestion has already been made by other writers that the Sea peoples may have included Nordic sailors, largely because the monument at Medinet Habu depicts some of them as men that look like Vikings. I must now express the view that the inscriptions have forced upon me: that I think it very probable that the Sea Peoples included substantial naval detachments from the Baltic region, that their language was a Nordic dialect of the Indo-European family, that the so-called "Libyan" alphabet is in fact an alphabet of Nordic or at least northern European origin, and that it was taken to Libya by the defeated Sea Peoples who survived the Battle of the Nile. For some reason the alphabet they introduced has continued in use throughout subsequent Libyan history, whereas in its northern homeland it died out, to be replaced by runes. I would also hazard the guess that the blond Tuaregs who clung most tenaciously to the "Libyan" alphabet are probably descended from Nordic immigrants around the time of the Sea Peoples' invasions. All these proposals may seem bold inferences, but I see little in the way of plausible alternatives in the light of these new finds of supposed Libyan inscriptions in Europe.

It is, after all, a question of relative motion. We thought at first that Libyan voyagers had traveled to Scandinavia, to leave their script there as a calling card. It now seems that the script is Nordic, and that Nordic ships and crews carried it to Libya, where it survived.

18

THE LANGUAGE OF OUR BRONZE AGE ANCESTORS

The English language is a member of the Teutonic family of tongues, to which belong also German and the Scandinavian languages. Until now the oldest examples of Teutonic language have been short runic texts from about the time of Christ.

King Woden-lithi's written version of his own tongue has given us the first decipherable information on how our ancestors spoke 4,000 years ago. With the aid of his American inscription, the fragmentary related inscriptions in the same alphabet, found in Scandinavia, can now also be deciphered, and they prove to be the same language as Woden-lithi's, or nearly so. Also, aided by this new information, we can now begin to solve the late Stone Age hieroglyphic rebus inscriptions. Adding these Neolithic forms to the alphabetic versions given us by Woden-lithi, one can now list some of the basic vocabulary of the Bronze Age Teutonic peoples. Here is a list made from the above sources. Words inferred from a Neolithic rebus are prefixed with an asterisk (*).

As written on stone	Pronunciation	Meaning	Related roots
a k w	akwe	deadly	Old English *acwellan* (slay)
a y	aye	ever, always	English *aye,* Old Norse *ei*
* ⅄ a	tha	gaze at	similar root in Icelandic
⅄ g, ⅄ gn	thag, thagen	day, days	root in all Teutonic tongues

As written on stone	Pronunciation	Meaning	Related roots
* ᚦ a g i	thagi	at dawn	Old English *daegred*
ᚦ m	thom	doom	Old English *dom*
ᚦ w r k	thwerk	dwarf	Norse *dvaerg,* dwarf
ᚦ r s i l	Thrasil	horse	Odin's magic horse-tree
f n r	Fenri	The giant wolf that attacked Tiw (god of war)	
gn gn n r	Gungnir	Magic hammer of the god Woden (Odin)	
gn n w	gnua	grind out	gnash
gn r ᚦ	gnireth	to thunder	
h k	hak	to strike	hack
h m r	hamr	hammer	root in all Teutonic languages
* h r n ᚦ	hrinda	to praise, worship	
* h r ng r	hringr	ring	same root in all Teutonic languages
* h r s a	hrosa	horse	Old German *ros,* Icelandic *hros*
h w l	hwal	whale	Norse *hval,* etc.
k gh	kogh	ship, "cog"	Norse *kogr.* This word also occurs on Swedish Bronze Age rock carvings
* k w i n a	kwina	woman	OE *cwen,* Modern English *queen*
* k w i s a n d	kwiesand	bent	similar word in Old Norse
k w n gn r	kunungr	king	Norse *konungr,* Old English *cyning*
* k y o l	kyol	keel	widespread Teutonic root
* k y o l n a k v i	kyol-nakwi	keeled ship	similar forms in Old Norse
l	la	lay	
l	lae	venom	
l th i	lithi	follower, servant	similar form in Norse

As written on stone	Pronunciation	Meaning	Related roots
l k k	likkya	body	similar in Old Norse
l l	lo, lo!	See and behold	Middle English *Lo!*
l n	Leon	Leo (constellation)	lion
l n	Luna	Moon	Latin *Luna* (used by Woden-lithi as a second name for *Mán,* moon goddess)
l w k	lukya	coils	similar root in Old Norse
l w m s	lumis	cunning	similar root in Icelandic
l z	letz	locked, trapped	similar root in Norse
m	mith	mid, middle	universal Indo-European root
m gn	magna	sorcery	magic
m k	maka	make	not in Old Norse; suggests a Saxon affinity
m l	mel	crush, grind	mill
m l	mal	measure	Scandinavian root same
m l n r	Molnir	Mjolnir, the magic hammer of Thunor (Thor)	
m n	man, men	man, men	universal Teutonic root
* m n	man, men	man, men	root inherited from Neolithic
m n	man	Moon	universal Teutonic and Indo-European root
m n	mand	hand	Lat. *manus,* Old Norse *mund*
* m n s kr	menneskr	person, people	Norse root
n m	nama	name	Anglo-Germanic, not Norse
n gh w	noghwi	ship	similar root in Old Norse
* n a t	nat	night	universal Teutonic root
n m	nema	take, hold	Old Norse root
n n ⅄	nantiv	approach	Old Norse root
n	nei	no, not	universal Teutonic root

As written on stone	Pronunciation	Meaning	Related roots
-n	-en, -inn	the	suffixed definite article, characteristic of Norse tongues
n w n	nefni	to name	Scandinavian form
ok, ek	ok,ek	and	Norse, and Old English *eac*
l, abbrev. for o l n	olna	forearm	ell (cloth measure)
r gh n	reghin	of the Gods	Old Norse form
r gh n	regin	rain	universal Teutonic form
r m l	ruml	rumble	in English and Old Norse
r m (and w r m)	orm, worm	serpent	universal Teutonic root
r n a r	runar	runes	Norse root "secret signs"
s l f n r	Slefnir	Woden's magic steed spawned by Loki	
s m r	sumar	summer	(word damaged, perhaps misread)
s w	swi(ka)	twisted, or, alternative-ly, venom-ous	Old Norse
Th n n o r, Th w n r	Thunor	Thor, thun-der	This is the Germanic form.
T i w, T w	Tiw	Tiw (god of war)	universal Teutonic
t m	tamr	tame	word as inscribed uncer-tain
t w n	twinnar	Gemini (Zodiacal twins)	universal Teutonic
w	we	protection	Norse root *vé* (occurs in prayers for safe voyages)
w	wo!	Woe! Be-ware:	formula in ancient curses.
w ⚡ n	Woden	Odin, Wo-den	Anglo-Germanic form of name Odin
w ⚡ n l th i	Woden-lithi	Servant of Woden	*lithi,* Norse form

As written on stone	Pronunciation	Meaning	Related roots
w ᛉ r (? a sky god)	Wether	sky, atmosphere, weather	
w f	wif	wife	Anglo-Saxon form of root
w gh	ugh(li)	fierce	Norse root, yielding English *ugly*
w gh - ᛉ r s i l	Ughdrasil	tree Yggdrasil (literally "fierce horse")	
w g n	Wagn	Ursa Major (Odin's wagon of Norse myth)	
w gn n	Wagn-en	Libra (Zodiac sign, literally "weigher")	
w gh	wig(r)	steed	a Norse form
w h l a	whula	wheel	Swedish *hjula,* wheel
w h l	whula	wheel (used by Woden-lithi for the wheeling of the wagon around the Pole)	
w l h l	Walhol	Valhalla	*Walhol* in Old Norse
w n	win, won	win, won	Anglo-Saxon form of root
w n r	Wanir	Earth gods	Norse form
w n r	Wenri	Fenri, giant wolf of Norse mythology	
w n t	wint(er)	winter	universal Teutonic root
w r	war, wer	was, were	universal Teutonic root
w r a	Freya	Freya	universal Teutonic goddess of fertility
w r ar	Freyr	Freyr	universal Teutonic god of fertility

As written on stone	Pronunciation	Meaning	Related roots
w r m	warm	warm	universal Teutonic root
w r m n	Worm-en	Scorpio ("the serpent"). Location in Zodiac suggests the special sense here.	
y m r	Ymir	the giant Himir	Norse mythology
y l m n	Yol-men	Yule clowns (as also shown in graphic form)	
y l	Yol	Yule (midwinter feasting, December 21)	
y l - n	Yol-en	the Yule	(definite article suffixed), a Norse feature.
y o m f (r)	Yomfru	Virgo (of Zodiac), the Maiden	Norse form
y s r	Ysir	Aesir sky gods	Etruscan, Latin, *Aesar;* Old Norse *Aesir.* Probably a Neolithic form

Pronunciation

King Woden-lithi's language was evidently pronounced with a strong pervading aspiration. Initial *r* is probably *hr.* Two signs for *r* appear in his alphabet. One of them is apparently to be rendered as *-ar,* or *-or.* The sign for *d* seems always to occur in words where Old Norse has ꝝ , a letter that also occurs in Old English; its sound is the *th* in words like *this, then.* The letter *t* appears in both unaspirated and aspirated forms. The aspirated form, here rendered as *th,* is to be pronounced as *th* in *with*.

Conclusions

Each year, as the field season ends and we return to examine and contemplate the results of our epigraphic expeditions, several outstanding facts become increasingly apparent.

One is that we have greatly underrated the achievements of the Bronze Age peoples of northern Europe. We have long known, from their conspicuous carvings that constitute the rock art of the Bronze Age, that the North Sea and the Baltic were the home waters of fleets of ships. What we have failed to realize is that those same ships, and characteristic Bronze Age style, are also depicted on the rocks and cliffs of the maritime regions of eastern North America. And now it is also apparent that these same matching petroglyphs, on both sides of the Atlantic, are also accompanied by readable texts cut in ancient scripts that are likewise found on either side of the Atlantic.

What this means, of course, is that the ancient shipwrights made sound vessels, whose skippers and crews sailed them across the ocean, thereby fulfilling their builders' dreams. Flotillas of ancient Norse, Baltic, and Celtic ships each summer set their prows to the northwest, to cross the Atlantic, to return later in the season with cargoes of raw materials furnished by the Algonquians with whom they traded. To make these crossings they depended in part upon the searoads that had been opened up by the amelioration of the climate at the peak of the Bronze Age. As oceanographers have inferred, the polar ice melted then, and the favorable westward-flowing air and water currents generated by the permanent polar high now became available to aid in the westward passage. The return voyage, as always, could be made on the west wind drift, in the latitude of around 40° north latitude, as Columbus rediscovered. While these Nordic traders opened up the northern parts of North America, other sailors from the Mediterranean lands were doing similar things (as I have recorded in *Saga America*), but their outward voyage lay along the path that Columbus employed, utilizing the westward-blowing trade winds, found at latitudes below 30° N.

Both sets of navigations, though employing different outward routes, were obliged to use the same homeward track, that of the westwind drift in middle latitudes. Along this common searoad the sailors of the two different regions would occasionally meet, thus prompting intercultural exchanges between the Baltic lands and North Africa, as I have inferred in this book.

At least twice since the close of the Stone Age, conditions have favored such events. The first occurred during the warm period of the middle Bronze Age, to which I have just referred. Then the world's climates cooled again, and the nothern route to America became too ice-bound and too dangerous to attract adventurers in that direction any longer. It remained thus until about A.D. 700, when once more the earth's climate ameliorated. Once again the northern icecap melted and the polar seas could support navigation that made use of the polar high. Once more mariners came to northeastern America, this time under a name by which they are known in history—the Vikings. Yet, as the inscriptions show, these Vikings were not just Norsemen; they included as before men from the Baltic lands, Lithuanians and Latvians, as well as Celts from Ireland and probably also Wales. After A.D. 1200 the earth grew colder again, the thousand vineyards of William the Conqueror's England died out, and Normans turned their attention to the south of Europe to bring in their Malmsey wines, no longer fermented in England, where no vineyards now survived. The old routes to America were deserted, and that western land lay ignored by Europe until the voyage of Columbus once more awakened the cupidity of monarchs who, by this time, now controlled large populations of Europe. This time the full force of European exploitation fell upon the Amerindians, and the age of American isolation had ended.

Another remarkable fact that is now impressing itself upon our minds is that the ancient Europeans were not barbarians. They not only spoke in the chief dialects of the Indo-European tongues, but already by late Neolithic times the Europeans *could write*. The languages they wrote now prove to have been comprehensible to us as representing the principal tongues of modern Europe: Teutonic, Baltic, Celtic, and also Basque. Yet another surprising discovery is due to Professor Linus Brunner, who announced in 1981 the occurrence of Semitic vocabulary in the newly identified Rhaetic language of ancient Switzerland.

The heretofore mysterious people, to whom the archaeologists have attached such names as "Beaker Folk," "Bell-beaker People," and so on, now prove to be Europeans of our own stocks, speaking—and writing—in early variant forms of languages that we can see are related closely to the classical Teutonic, Celtic, and other tongues of Europe at the time of the Romans. The inscriptions found on their artifacts prove this. That it was not understood before is simply because archaeologists have mistaken the writing for decorative engraving. When a loom weight has inscribed upon it the word *warp,* it is quite obvious that this is a purely practical identification label for a weaver. Decorative it may be, but let us not overlook the fact that such a label tells us immediately the linguistic stock of the person who engraved it. And, of course, it also certifies that the ancient engraver belonged to a literate society.

The same is true of the engravers of the rock and cliff inscriptions of Scandinavia. When we discover that the "meaningless decoration" beside their ship carvings is none other than a readable comment in Baltic speech, appropriate to the scene depicted, we know at once that the designer was familiar with the language spoken by the ancestors of the people who still live along the Baltic coasts today. They were, in short, Balts. Let us recognize this simple fact, and call them by their proper names. And when we find very similar, and similarly lettered, engravings on North America rocks, it is our obligation to our ancestors to recognize their European origins, and to call them by their proper names too.

Yet another of the new facts now coming to our attention is the surprising discovery that words appropriate to the contexts are painted or engraved beside the famous cavern paintings of the great Aurignacian sites of Europe. These works of art have been attributed to Palaeolithic people of 20,000 years ago, yet we find now that they apparently used the same words for the animals they painted as did German and French, Spanish and Basque speakers within historic times. When a German of the Middle Ages called a wild bison a *wisent,* he was using the same word that we find written in Baltic script beside one of the most famous ancient paintings of a bison, that on the roof of the Altamira Cavern.

Other paintings in other caves are similarly accompanied by ogam or Baltic script, rendering the names of the animals in tongues of the Celtic and Basque families. We do not find such inscriptions beside paintings of animals that disappeared from Europe during the last glaciation. Thus the mammoths are not identified by name (though the Basque word that means "Bogeyman" appears beside one such mammoth picture). I think this means that the paintings were added in sequence over a long period of time, and only the latest of the series carry identifications in written language. Thus I think it is wrong to date all the parietal art to about 20,000 B.C. That part of it that carries readable labels must be much younger.

In proof of the truth of this contention I may cite the case of the Basque bone disk "coinage," mentioned in Chapter 15. This is obviously a local Pyrenean copy, made by Basques from a silver model provided by the Celtic coins of Aquitania in the second century before Christ. We have to correct the dating assigned by archaeologists, for it is not 20,000 years old, but only 2,000 years of age, and its purpose was not that of a bead or a button, but that of token coinage. The word engraved on it is still used in present-day Basque.

Thus, the forthcoming years will doubtless witness more drastic pruning of the antiquity assigned to some European works of art. They may have been the work of Paleolithic hunters but, if so, then the Paleolithic way of life as hunters and food-gatherers must have persisted in some parts of Europe well into the era that is generally called late Neolithic. In the world today there are still Stone Age peoples. So also in Europe in the Bronze Age, 3,000 years ago, there may well have been pockets of isolated people, living in the Paleolithic manner but acquainted with the writing systems used by their more civilized neighbors, and applying it to the labeling of their art work.

We have been slow to recognize the presence of written words in the Celtic, Basque, and Teutonic tongues beside or on these ancient cave paintings. But since we have begun to read the inscriptions, the time has come to reconsider the role of linguists in archaeology.

Have we, perhaps, devoted too much attention to the grammatical niceties of ancient languages, and not enough to the daily vocabulary of the simple country people who really constituted the bulk of the population in classical times? I think that too many published papers appear with titles like "On the Use of the Optative Mood in Aeolic Greek after the Time of Alcaeus." Many more papers ought to be written under headings such as "The Vocabulary of Six Greek Graffiti from a Mycenaean Village."

Grammar without vocabulary is useless. Vocabulary without grammar is decidedly useful. With a slight knowledge, and dreadful pronunciation, of Berber, I was able in North Africa to elicit friendship and valuable aid during my North African work. Elegant Arabic, however literary and grammatical, would not have availed so well as a few uttered words of Berber that I had recognized as belonging to the Indo-European vocabulary of ancient Europe. The white Berbers have no recollection of their ancestors' having come from Europe, yet their anatomy declares them to be Europoids. Their vocabulary also yields European roots, whereas their grammar tells us nothing about the origin of their language.

During Norman times the English tongue was shorn of nearly all its characteristic Teutonic grammar, and instead a simplified Anglo-French set of grammatical rules took its place. On the other hand, the vocabulary retained most of the old Saxon roots, and added much French and Latin to them. To modern students from Asia, English seems to be (as one of them described it to me) "a kind of French." His ideas were based on shared vocabulary and such grammatical features as the use by modern English of the French plural in a terminal -s, almost all the old Teutonic plurals in -n having disappeared, except in rural dialects. A farmer still makes *kine* the plural of *cow,* but the city dweller does not. So it is from the farmers and other village folk that we can get best information on the older forms of European languages.

This is a general rule. When Sir Henry Rawlinson set about the—seemingly hopeless—task of deciphering the cliff-cut cuneiform inscriptions of Behistun, he made the basic premise that the tongue of the local Iranian villagers might be the closest he could find to the language of the ancient inscription cut by Darius. Just as Champollion used Coptic to guide him into ancient Egyptian, so also Rawlinson used the local idioms of Behistun itself. These approaches, which sound naive, are in fact well founded on reason, and they produced results.

I hope that a younger generation of linguists will arise from our hidebound universities, and turn once more, as Jakob Grimm did a century ago, to the village communities of Europe. Let them collect the old vocabulary and discover whatever words they can, however vulgar they may seem to the city ear. It is from these ancient words that we shall garner the most useful guides to the speech of our ancestors 5,000 years ago. Much that Julius Pokorny has done, by way of extracting the "highest common factor" from each set of related Indo-European words, has helped in reading the old inscriptions. He and his predecessors and his successors, such as Linus Brunner and Imanol Agife, are worthy explorers of the tongues of our ancestors. The inscribed artifacts of Stone Age people also bear information that has been overlooked.

It is not a random harvest, but one already partly organized. The harvest is ripe for the gathering, and now is the time to bring it in.

GLOSSARY

The following terms are used frequently in the literature of Bronze Age archaeology, linguistics, and mythology. This list may serve as a handy reference.

Aesir Sky gods, chiefly Woden, Tiw, Thunor, and Loki, introduced into North American contexts ca. 1700 B.C. from either northern Germany or southern Denmark.

Aquitania District in southwest France, adjacent to the Basque provinces, where an ogam consaine coinage in silver was struck in the second century B.C., carrying the Celtic word *nomse* and modeled on the Greek coinage, *nomisma,* issued by the nearby town of Emporion. *See* ogam, ogam consaine.

barrow An earth mound, usually circular in America, covering one or more human burials.

boustrophedon Term of Greek origin used for Bronze Age script that runs alternately from right to left and left to right, like a plowman's furrow. The term means literally "walking like a plow-ox."

brachycephalic Adjective meaning skulls of rounded type. Seen in most North American Indians, Asiatic peoples, and the peoples of central Europe.

Byanu (and similar spellings) Mother goddess of the Gadelic Celts, worshipped at Windmill Hill, Britain, ca. 2000 B.C. and in North America, as ogam consaine inscriptions at both extremities of the range disclose. See my *America B.C.*

cairns or carns Mounds of stones, sometimes covering burials, sometimes serving as way guides or as sighting points in calendar regulation by the sunrise position.

capstone The uppermost slab of stone, or a boulder, covering a dolmen or a part of a stone chamber, extending from side to side, without corbeling.

cog An oceangoing Norse trading ship. Used by the Ontario Nordic settlers, who called it *kogh* in their inscriptions.

consonantal script Typical writing of the Bronze Age in which only the consonants are expressed, the vowels being supplied by the reader with the help of the context.

corbeling Method of roofing a stone chamber in which each successive tier of stones overhangs the tier below and projects inward, so that ultimately a tier is reached at which the overhanging stones all meet at the center, producing an arched ceiling. Used where large capstones are not available.

Creole language Any tongue that has developed from the fusion of two or more languages. (A term used professionally, not yet assimilated into vernacular English.) Middle English and many North American languages are examples. Another term, preferred by some linguists, is *Mischsprache* (German, "mixed language").

cromlech A megalithic tomb in which a large capstone and several vertical stones supporting it and concealing a burial has become exposed through erosion of the original earth covering. Some dolmens may originally have been earth-covered, and could therefore be called cromlechs.

determinative (also called *classifier*) A small pictograph supplied by a Bronze Age scribe in words where the consonants alone may not suffice to disclose the word intended. It indicates the category of a word: e.g., "brother" is a member of the category "men."

disk barrow A low circular earth mound containing one or many burials, usually females. Typical in Europe of the early Bronze Age. They occur in New England.

dolichocephalic Adjective meaning long-headed, applied to skulls where the cranium is relatively long compared to its width, as in many people who live on the western borders of Europe, or who descend from such stock. *See* brachycephalic.

dolmen Megalithic monument in which a capstone of up to 90 tons stands supported on three or more vertical stones. Large examples appear to have been monuments in honor of a deceased chief; perhaps sometimes also used for religious gatherings. Smaller examples are considered to be the internal chamber of a burial, exposed through erosion of the earth. *See* cromlech.

druid Member of the Celtic pagan priesthood.

druid's chair Term used in New England for megalithic rock thrones, adapted for use from naturally occurring boulders of appropriate shape.

dysse Scandinavian term for dolmen.

Gadelic Celts Celts who spoke a language related to Gaelic, and who came to Britain from the Rhineland around 2200 B.C. They built Stonehenge and their inscriptions from Windmill Hill show them to have written their language in ogam consaine, similar to that of New England. In Britain they are called Beaker People.

gorget A neck or breast ornament. Ogam and Iberic inscriptions cut on some bear out the true nature of some crude stones so identified as being loom weights, for holding warp threads taut.

grave goods Articles buried with the dead. If inscribed in a readable script, they disclose the linguistic relations of the deceased or of peoples with whom trade was carried on.

hella A flat rock platform; often used for Norse inscriptions.

henge A circular enclosed area, surrounded by an earthen mound or by large stones, constructed in Europe at the end of the Neolithic period, 2500 to 2000 B.C., but continuing in use into Bronze Age times. Presumably for religious and astronomical purposes. North American stone rings in some cases may have been henges.

Hjulatorp The locality in Sweden where Nordic words for *wheel* and *globe* occur in ogam and Bronze Age runes ("Libyan Tifinag") beside engravings of wheels and globes, dated to the Scandinavian Bronze Age. Also applied to similar localities.

intrusive burial A later burial inserted into an ancient barrow and therefore accompanied sometimes by grave goods inappropriate to the era of construction of the barrow.

Iron Age The period when iron replaced bronze as the principal metal. In northern Europe it lasted from about 700 B.C. until Roman times.

jaettestue Scandinavian term meaning "giant's salon." Applied to megalithic chambers of the Bronze Age and late Neolithic.

Jol or Yul Yule, the midwinter pagan festival of the Nordic peoples.

Jol-man or Yul-man A clown featured in the midwinter festival of the Nordic colony in Ontario.

Lex Coloniae. Decree issued by the Roman Senate in 133 B.C., forbidding (among other things) the use on Iberian coinage of ogam or Iberic scripts. Temporarily revoked by Augustus in A.D. 2, when an ogam consaine coinage celebrated the adoption by Augustus of Lucius Caesar as his heir.

loathsome runes Term used by nonliterate Norse, fearful that written inscriptions might contain a curse.

loom weights   Small stones with one or two holes, used for keeping warp threads taut on the vertical loom of Scandinavian and Iberian type. Ogam and Iberic inscriptions on North American examples identify their purpose. Usually called "gorgets" in North America. *See* gorget.

Lug   Gadelic Celtic god of light. In North America, introduced by the Celtiberians but later fused with the Nordic Woden.

Mabon   Gadelic Celtic god of music, sports, and fertility of males. In North America later fused with Freyr and named in younger runes, but by his Celtic name.

megalithic   Term applied to structures built of large stone blocks, without mortar, usually religious or burial chambers, standing stones and dolmens.

menhir   Synonym for *sarsen*.

mesocephalic   Referring to skulls intermediate between long- and round-headed types.

mesognathous   Jaws intermediate between orthognathous and prognathous types.

nokkvi or noghwi   Ancient Nordic and later Norse term for a ship. Used in Bronze Age inscriptions in North America and Scandinavia as a term for the sky-ship of the sun god and moon goddess and also for ordinary seagoing craft.

Nordic   Any member of any tongue of the group that includes the related Norse, Germanic, English, and Gothic peoples and languages.

ogam   A system of writing employing combinations of up to five parallel strokes set on a "stem" line. An ancient writing system ranging back to at least the Bronze Age. *See* Aquitania.

ogam consaine   Consonantal ogam, not employing vowels. Used in Swedish Bronze Age inscriptions in conjunction with Bronze Age runes, in the Basque provinces at least as early as the second century B.C., also in France, in North America throughout the first millennium B.C., and thereafter to modern times.

orthognathous   Term applied to skulls in which the chin is well developed and the teeth form a vertical, not a projecting, border to the mouth.

orthostats   Large flat slabs of stone sometimes used to form the walls and entrance of megalithic chambers.

Ostre or Eostre   A goddess of the dawn of the Germans and English, lacking from Scandinavia. Celebration of the spring equinox (Easter) by Woden-lithi's colonists marked the beginning of the new year and planting of crops.

petroglyph   Any inscription or picture cut in rock.

phonoglyph   Any carved letter that conveys a sound, as in modern alphabets.

potsherd   A broken pottery fragment. They are often used in classifying archaeological sites.

prognathous   Term applied to skulls in which the teeth and jaws project.

Regin-Domr   "Doom of the Gods," the end of the world, as depicted in King Woden-lithi's inscriptions.

rain god   A sky god, called Taran or Daran by the Celts, Thunor by the Ontario Nordic people of Woden-lithi, and corresponding to Thor and Jupiter. Rock-cut inscriptions in North America name the god in both languages.

runes (Old Norse *runar,* secret writing)   Term applied to any Nordic script, from the fact that originally the Nordic scribes were wizards who did not disclose to commoners the meaning of the letters.

sarsen   Term used in southwest Britain for natural stone elongate slabs that have been erected vertically by human agency, either singly or in groups. Also called phallic monuments, and supposedly the sites of fertility ceremonies.

spatulate or "shovel-shaped"   Term applied to the upper incisor teeth of many North American Indians and Asiatic peoples. The characteristic is ancient, and occurs in the Australopithecine apemen of Africa, in Neanderthals, in Asian Paleolithic people, and in a proportion of the population in many other races. The characteristic is rare in Europe and in Negroid races.

suffix-article   Linguistic term for the definite article suffixed to its noun, a characteristic feature of the Scandinavian tongues. The suffix-article occurs as a Norse aspect of the language of King Woden-lithi in Ontario, ca. 1700 B.C.

trilithon   Two upright stones with a third lying horizontally across them. In the midwestern and western states they seem to take the place of the eastern dolmens, where three or more uprights support the capstone. At Stonehenge a group of trilithons occurs, in which the capstone is smaller than the uprights. In North America only solitary examples are known, and the capstone is much larger than the uprights.

Walhol   The sky residence of the Aesir in Woden-lithi's mythology. It corresponds to Valhalla of the Norsemen.

Wanir   Earth gods, chiefly Freyr and Freya, relating to fertility, and introduced to North America ca. 1700 B.C. from north Germany or southern Denmark. *See* Aesir.

Woden-lithi   A Nordic king, perhaps of Jutish origin, who established a trading colony in Ontario ca. 1700 B.C. The name means "Servant of Odin."

Ymir   A sea-dwelling giant of Nordic mythology (*Himir* in Norse), recorded in King Woden-lithi's Ontario inscriptions.

younger runes   Norse script in use after ca. A.D. 1000. It appears in rock scripts in North America, notably as identification labels on Celtic gods such as Lug and Mabon.

INDEX